House Plants and Indoor Gardening

House Plants and Indoor Gardening

Cyril C Harris

Octopus Books

First published 1973 by
Octopus Books Limited
59 Grosvenor Street, London, W.1

ISBN O 7064 0115 8
© 1973 Octopus Books Limited

Produced by Mandarin Publishers
14 Westlands Road, Quarry Bay, Hong Kong
and printed in Hong Kong

Contents

Introduction

Growing and displaying plants indoors has been popular for many generations. Particularly during the seventeenth, eighteenth and nineteenth centuries, people adorned their houses with exotic plants, in some cases sponsoring plant explorers to travel far afield to collect specimens for them. During the nineteenth century interest in plants waned, but about twenty years ago everything changed, and house plants became popular again in every walk of life to an extent greater than ever before.

The purposes to which house plants are put and the motives for possessing and caring for them, are manifold. Sometimes it is their exceptional value in interior decor, which may or may not be inspired by an interest in growing them; then there is that almost primitive urge to cultivate, which exists in so many human beings, who derive satisfaction from bringing their gardening adventures, especially in the winter, into the comfortable environment of their homes; there are others who, haunted by a sense of deprivation because they have no garden, find that in house plants they can enjoy the interest they have yearned for; and, finally, there are the connoisseurs who find great joy in accepting the challenge that growing the more delicate and difficult subjects offers them.

It is hoped that to a greater or lesser degree this book will be a help to all of them.

Choosing Indoor Plants

As a preliminary to choosing and growing indoor plants, it is important to spend a little time considering the different types of plants that are available. Firstly, house plants can be described as those plants that give a permanent display throughout the year. They are always green and do not have a resting period like many other plants. Some house plants are attractive because of the beautiful colour and form of their foliage, while others, fewer in number, add to this loveliness by flowering. It might be usefully mentioned that although quite a number of them have common names, many are offered by florists under their somewhat frightening botanical names. Do not, however, be put off by this, because they are quite easy to learn. In fact, it is often safer to use the Latin description because, in some instances, the common names are duplicated.

The second category of indoor plants that feature nowadays quite prominently, includes what are known as 'flowering pot plants', which are characterized by the fact that they have resting periods, during which, in most cases, they become quite uninteresting. Popular examples of this group are Indian azaleas, astilbe, calceolaria, chrysanthemums, cineraria, cyclamen, Cape heaths, hydrangeas and primulas.

Other very attractive plants grown indoors are cacti, succulents, ferns and palms, and those from bulbs. In addition, there are the fascinating and often beautiful miniature and bonsai trees. These can very attractively supplement the décor of a room and for the garden minded, raising and training them is an intriguing hobby.

When buying for indoors, the three most important considerations are (1) the conditions under which they are to grow, (2) the purpose to which they are to be put and (3) the experience of the owner and the amount of time that can be devoted to their proper upkeep. There can be little doubt that many casualties among house plants have occurred because gift plants, given all in good faith, have not had these factors taken into account.

There are quite a number of things to be considered, such as the amount of light in the room, whether it is centrally or permanently heated, whether there are periods when it is cold, whether a plant is required for a permanently cold place, possibly a hall, or for a continuously sunny spot, and so

on. Equally important is the purpose for which it is needed. A plant for a small table or an office desk must be compact and bushy, whereas a climber is needed for a room divider. Does a house plant that flowers or a foliage plant with coloured or variegated leaves serve the purpose best? It could be that, for some reason, possibly connected with the décor or the immediate view from the window of the room, colour changes are needed from season to season, in which case it is possible that bulbs and flowering pot plants are more appropriate. Lastly, there are several foliage plants that can easily spare some of their leaves. These might be invaluable to flower arrangers at a time when suitable foliage is scarce out of doors.

The choice of a house plant might be materially influenced by the circumstances of its owner. If a beginner, easy-to-grow plants are recommended until some knowledge has been gained. The more experienced could undoubtedly be more venturesome and grow the delicate and difficult plants, and perhaps ultimately turn a hand to propagation. Much must depend, even with the most expert, on the amount of time that can be devoted to the maintenance of house plants. A busy business woman might easily find that she must limit her choice to the easy-to-grow and more hardy varieties. If there are periodical absences from home, it might be that cacti are the best choice. Providing they have plenty of sunshine and are not exposed to frost, they will exist quite happily at a temperature of 45–50°F (7–10°C) and with comparatively little water from late summer to spring.

There is one rather more unusual form of indoor plant which is mentioned at this point, because logically it does not fit anywhere else in this book. This is a miniature water-lily, growing in a large bowl, at least twelve inches in diameter. An excellent variety for this purpose is *Pygmaea helvola*, which is a very beautiful bright yellow. If it is planted in a box made from a piece of pretty, small-mesh plastic or metal netting, filled with good garden soil, which preferably contains a little clay rather than one on the sandy side, it will flourish with very little attention, particularly if it is put on a sunny window-sill.

Finally, when buying always go to a reputable nurseryman or florist, if possible in your district, so that there is little risk

Traditional and newly cultivated
indoor plants (below)

A plant group cultivated with the
aid of modern conditions (right)

of damage when you transport plants home. A good grower will always harden off his plants, which have been raised in the warm, humid environment of his greenhouse, before he sells them to a flower shop or to a retail customer. An efficient florist will, in turn, look after the plants that have been delivered, they will be watered and kept out of draughts and they certainly will not be exposed to hot sunshine or cold winds out of doors.

It is always advisable to buy house plants, particularly the more delicate ones, in the summer, autumn or during a mild spell, so that they do not suffer any shock on being carried home on a cold, windy day. You should at any time make sure that any house plant is well wrapped to protect it on its homeward journey. You can be sure that a good florist or nurseryman will know exactly how to do this.

When making a choice, you should always pick out a plant with firm, brightly coloured foliage and without any pests, since these will not only damage this plant, but will also infest any that you have already at home. Particularly see that there is no damaged foliage, especially with those plants that depend upon their leaves for their beauty, such as *Ficus elastica* 'Decora', *Fatsia japonica* and *Monstera deliciosa*.

After it has been brought home, any house plant should be treated very kindly for the first week or so. It should be watered with luke-warm water, but only if necessary, and put into a warm place, out of draughts and full sun, to dry. Be careful you do not give it too much heat or water. After about a week it can be placed in its permanent quarters and treated normally, but it should be watched for another four weeks until there are signs that it is happy, which it usually signifies by some growth.

In the appendix there is an At-A-Glance Guide that will assist in the selection of house plants for several different conditions. These plants are described on pages 33—73.

Using Plants in the House

There are so many varieties in shape, colour and living conditions relating to indoor plants that it is possible to find something for every situation in the house. They can be acclaimed not only for their beauty, but for their utilitarian aspects. Among the latter, mention must be made of the immense value of the climbing plants in making room dividers. These are most applicable to living quarters designed on the open plan. One very practical device is a light screen, made by training, say, *Ficus pumila* or any of the ivies, for separating the drawing- and dining-room areas of a room, in which the contrast between the dining furniture and that of the living-room might be quite incongruous. It might equally well serve as a screen to conceal the remnants of a meal when entertaining. Sometimes there is a place for a much denser divider, in which case *Cissus antarctica, Philodendron scandens* or *Tetrastigma voinierianum* might be excellent subjects. In a modern bed-sitter, such a plant might, for example, make a very attractive barrier between the living section and the sleeping quarters, or it might hide from view the cooking utensils. From a more aesthetic angle, climbers can be beautiful if they are allowed to frame a window.

In a house with a garden, the view of the garden from the window is probably one of its most treasured features. Many who live in a flat or a house in a town are deprived of this joy. It is possible, however, to capture some of this lost pleasure with indoor plants. Two or three of them, of varying heights, growing on the window-sill, will produce a delightful effect. The more ambitious plant grower might even replace the window-sill with a full-length trough and make an indoor garden. In this case a venetian blind should be set to exclude both sun and frost. House plants can be used to hide an empty fireplace during the summer, or all the year round in houses where central heating has been installed. The chimney, however, should be blocked with a piece of cardboard or hardboard, particularly during the winter, to prevent the cold draughts from damaging the plants. It should always be remembered that being situated away from the window, they are in a dark place, so plants requiring less light should be used, or, far more delightful, the display should be illuminated with a spotlight.

Even as part of interior decoration, indoor plants have

some practical uses. They may be valuable tools in the hands of the designer, especially in contemporary houses, where they can do much to soften some of the starkness of much modern building. An unembellished white wall, for example, can be transformed by a single specimen of *Ficus elastica* 'Decora' in the foreground. The lofty ceilings of an elegant drawing-room can be optically lowered by the presence of a spreading *Philodendron selloum.* An arrangement of colourful house plants, lit with fluorescent bulbs, can turn a dark corner into a light, bright environment. Climbing plants carefully trained to break up the surface can also bring beauty and relief to an undesirable expanse of empty wall; in addition, the gaunt balustrades of an ill-designed staircase can be hidden by the verdure of their fresh leaves. Another excellent way of giving relief and interest to empty walls is to fix suitable containers on brackets on them, and plant both bushy and trailing horse plants in these.

The many shapes, sizes and colours of house plants give enormous scope to interior designers to meet the personal tastes of almost all their clients. They enliven and bring great charm to a room and do much to finish off with perfection many décor schemes. They can be most successfully accompanied by the many flowering pot plants to give cheerfulness to any room in the depths of winter, when everything outside is dreary. On hot days, by contrast, they can bring a freshness and light-hearted gayness. Again, the large, shiny, rich green surfaces of the leaves and their boldness of design, like those of some of the philodendrons, *Monstera deliciosa* and *Fatsia japonica,* can lessen the fussiness of a small fabric design, while the small-leaved and variegated foliage of other plants can do much to relieve effectively the starkness of curtains and soft furnishings in plain materials. These are but a few ways in which interior decorators can turn their ingenuity to using these very beautiful plants.

Be warned, however: the use of house plants must not be overdone. The dedicated indoor gardener is recommended to set aside a spare room, amply lit with fluorescent lighting, for his hobby. In the house, generally, indoor plants must be kept under control and used with imagination. They should accent a room, but not become the main feature.

Perhaps some of the most fascinating of displays are pro-

Many types of containers and troughs are suitable for a dish or trough garden. A pleasant trip around the antique or junk shops, according to the depth of your purse, might produce the ideal container; perhaps it would be a soup tureen, a washhand basin or a copper preserving pan, while the modern boutiques can often supply wooden troughs, ones made of basketwork and wrought-iron ones with a metal lining. Sometimes conical baskets or clay dishes mounted on contemporary designed wrought-iron legs or other fascinating vessels suitable for indoor gardens, can be procured. Even the pedestal vases, that are so popular with flower arrangers, can be used to make the loveliest miniatures.

Then there is, of course, the specimen house plant growing in its individual pot, in which it can be seen at its very best, and which certainly does most of all to give accent to the décor. But whatever is chosen as a container for a single plant or a grouping must not detract from the beauty of the plant itself. Indeed, how often does one see a house plant at its very loveliest in a humble clay pot!

The manner in which house plants are displayed is vitally important to the décor of any room. There are glass-top wrought-iron tables, corner stands with several shelves, and other furniture of modern design. And, it is amazing how oldfashioned furniture, such as long abandoned corner washstands (if possible complete with utensils), whatnots, three-tier round tables and those monstrosities, such as brass and mahogany pot stands in which our Edwardian forebears flaunted their aspidistras, are so miraculously resuscitated when their woods of walnut, mahogany and rosewood mingle with the soft, fresh foliage of our present-day house plants.

cured in bottle (carboy) gardens and terrariums, in which the plants grow in a totally enclosed atmosphere. The making of such gardens is described on page 127-31. It needs some skill and is an intriguing hobby, for the results are very lovely and attract much attention. One very effective way of utilizing a bottle garden is to convert the bottle (after it has been planted out) into a table lamp, making sure that the plants are still accessible for future care. This use certainly ensures that the plants will be well lit. Bottle gardens can be employed to fill an empty corner, or to be stood on a table, and can be very effective at the head of a staircase, where their details can be observed by anybody mounting the stairs.

Some people like to grow their house plants in miniature gardens in which are incorporated diminutive garden features, such as paths, pools (made of mirror), lawns of mossy plants, bridges, etc. Sometimes cacti are planted instead of house plants, but it is unwise to mix them. Constructing a miniature garden can be both fascinating and instructive, especially for a child, see page 127.

Dish gardens and troughs are a favourite way of growing indoor plants. These are also discussed in greater detail on page 127. Here it is sufficient to say that the choice of plants for this purpose is extremely important. They must all like the same growing conditions. To be aesthetically pleasing, the selection must include plants of varying heights, with a taller one as a leader; and they must be more or less equally vigorous so that none over-runs its neighbours. An interesting, more recently introduced innovation is to sink into the compost glass or metallic florist's tubes, which allow the inclusion of cut flowers to give continued interest and increased beauty.

Philodendron Bipennifolium:
a suitable, hardy plant for an
office

Using Plants in the Office

Office plants, ranging from massive displays in the main entrance to the individual pot on the top of a filing cabinet, are becoming increasingly popular. Many reasons have been advanced to conscientious office managers and house plant maintenance contractors to explain why house plants are a justifiable expense in a commercial concern. Probably, however, the most cogent, but perhaps more nebulous, reason for their use is that they make the office a pleasanter place in which to work.

From a utilitarian point of view, the everchanging moods of plants can soften the décor of many modern offices and mask the somewhat harsh lines of contemporary office furniture. More important, climbing plants can form relatively low space-consuming divisions in open-plan offices, as experience has shown that movement of persons is far more disturbing to personnel than machine noise. Climbing house plants and larger specimens can also be very effectively employed as screens behind which to hide temporary piles of incoming goods awaiting removal to storage. It could also be argued that their presence is an aid to tidiness.

It might be claimed by some that the presence of plants can have a good psychological influence on office workers. Certainly, those who are gardeners would appreciate them; for a long time it has been recognized that green is a restful colour. Moreover, in cities they are a pleasing contrast to the starkness and shabbiness of the brick-buildings seen through the office windows.

The greatest problem of having house plants in offices is their upkeep: How are they to be tended during hot weekends and holiday periods when the self-appointed, dedicated, office plant-lover is away? The answer, no doubt, is that the managing director should engage a house plant contractor to handle this problem for him. The contractor is a specialist and knows the most suitable plants for the purpose, what attention they need and when failing plants should be replaced.

For those who are interested in using the services available for this purpose, an outline of two types of contracts are given very briefly in the ensuing paragraphs.

Under one scheme the commercial concern buys and owns the plants and arranges with a contractor, who is usually the supplier, to maintain them regularly, about once a week. When plants need replacing the contractor undertakes to advise the owner. The great disadvantage of this type of contract is that, because of expense, there is often reluctance on the part of both parties to make the necessary replacements frequently enough and the display becomes shabby.

Under another rather more satisfactory arrangement, the contractor hires out the plants and agrees to maintain them regularly. In addition, he also contracts to replace immediately any plants that are failing. Under this type of agreement, arrangements in private offices are also regularly replaced so that interest is sustained and dying and overgrown dish gardens dealt with. In addition, when it is desired, the contractor will hire out bowls, dishes and other containers, and self-watering devices.

Suitable House Plants for Offices

Finding the right type of plants for an office is quite a problem and one best left to the expert. Probably the greatest menace can be the house plant that has found its way into the office through a good-hearted collection for somebody's birthday. Usually, unwittingly, the plant chosen is totally unsuited to the conditions under which it has to live and after a week or so it becomes a sordid object, instead of the thing of beauty that it should be. There is little doubt that only the toughest plant can survive and live happily in the atmosphere that even a modern office block has to offer. Although most offices do not suffer from the problem of insufficient light, there are other hazards. Excessive heat, hot radiators, dry air, draughts, tobacco smoke, deposits of unwanted vending-machine coffee and baking sun are but a few that can play havoc with the toughest specimens.

House plant suppliers and contractors have, however, learnt a lot about suitable house plants for this purpose. On page 29 is a list, that has been compiled by a leading house plant nurseryman, of those he has found to be most satisfactory. He has graded them according to his assessment of their suitability. Those in Grade 1 are excellent; those in Grade 2 very good; and those in Grade 3 are good and satisfactory. Peperomias are used for infilling in arrangements for the first six months until the other members have grown.

Totem pole Philodendron (left)

Climbers and trailers mixed (right)

An arrangement for an office hallway

Suitable House Plants for Offices

Grade 1

Pandanus veitchii
Sansevieria trifasciata 'Laurentii'

Grade 2

Aechmea fasciata
Ananas bracteatus 'Striata'
Billbergia nutans
B. windii
Chamaedorea elegans
Chlorophytum elatum 'Variegatum'
Dieffenbachias
Dracaena deremensis 'Warnecki'
D. godseffiana
D. sanderiana
D. marginata
D. volckaerti
Ficus elastica 'Decora'
Maranta 'Tricolor'

Monstera deliciosa
Philodendron bipennifolium
P. 'Burgundy'
P. hastatum
P. laciniatum
P. pertusum
P. scandens
P. tuxia
Schefflera actinophylla
Scindapsus aureus
Spathiphyllum 'Mauna Loa'
S. wallisii
Syngonium podophyllum
S. podophyllum 'Emerald Gem'
S. vellozianum

Grade 3

Aechmea fasciata
Aeschyanthus speciosus
Anthurium scherzerianum
Aralia (Dizygotheca) elegantissima
Asplenium nidus avis
Cocos weddelliana
Cryptanthus
Ctenanthe lubbersiana
Ficus australis
F. benjamina
F. doecheri
F. pumila
F. schryveriana
Guzmania lingulata 'Minor Flambea'

Gynura sarmentosa
* Hibiscus rosa-sinensis 'Cooperi'
Hoya carnosa
Kentia forsteriana (Howea)
Maranta leuconeura 'Kerchoveana'
Neoregelia carolinae
N. marechali
Philodendron fenzlii
P. selloum
Platycerium alcicorne
Rhoicissus rhomboidea
Saxifraga sarmentosa
Scindapsus pictus 'Argyraeus'
Tolmiea menziesii

* requires good light

Philodendron Burgundy (right)
Hedera Helix Adam (below left)
Monstera Deliciosa, showing
aerial roots (below right)

Climbing and Trailing Foliage Plants

Already on pages 9–15 a guide has been given as to the various uses to which house plants can be put and the different growing conditions which are acceptable to them. In this and the next chapter, foliage house plants are described in greater detail. Quite a large proportion of the house plants available in these days are climbers or trailers or both. The present chapter is devoted to this category.

Training and Supporting Climbers

Although some climbing house plants can be quite effectively used as trailers and included in arrangements in hanging baskets, if they are to be effective as climbers they need some sort of support over which they can clamber. Some plants are self-clinging, but most of them have to be tied. When this is necessary, it is important to see that the ties are not so tight that they restrict growth. There are some quite good plastic and paper-covered wire ties and plastic-covered wire rings on the market. These are very good in the case of plants with heavy foliage which keeps them out of sight. In the ordinary way, brown or green string, tied lightly to the support and then loosely round the stem (using a reef knot in both cases), is quite satisfactory.

Some plants, including a few of the Philodendrons, Scindapsus, and the upright growing *Monstera deliciosa*, produce roots from the stems above ground level. It is advantageous if such plants are provided with a support to which these aerial roots, as they are termed, can cling from which they can draw supplies of water. Such a support, which is known as a moss stick or totem pole, will be described later.

Returning to the first type of climber, which does not produce aerial roots, most of these can be supported by means of canes. In the case of climbers such as ivy, support can be given adequately with a framework formed by inserting three canes at the points of an isosceles triangle at the edge of the pot (see Figure 1, page 34). For stability the stakes should be driven in almost to the bottom of the container. The plants can be effectively trained round such a structure.

Sometimes it is more effective to make a trellis by driving well into the soil canes, set at a slight angle, across the centre of the pot. Then cross-members, consisting of split canes, are lashed to these uprights at intervals of about 4½ inches by

means of thin wire (see Figure 2, page 34).

In order to make a moss stick or totem pole, it is necessary to obtain from the hardware store some ¼-inch plastic mesh, which is 30 or 36 inches wide. A strip of this is cut off across the width of such a piece, so that when it is rolled it forms a cylinder about 2½ to 3 inches in diameter, when its edges are overlapped by about ¾ inch. These are fastened at intervals of about 6 inches with wire. The cylinder is made more rigid by inserting two sticks, with a square cross-section of such an area that they are held in position by the plastic fabric, through the mesh near the bottom of the cylinder, at right angles to each other. The latter is then stood on the crocks in the container. Next the cylinder is filled to about three or four inches from the top with a mixture of shredded moss and vermiculite or similar material, mixed in about equal proportions. While this is being done, the mixture should be consolidated with the end of a broom handle. The shredded moss should have been well moistened by soaking it during the previous sixteen to twenty-four hours. A sufficiently thick layer of soil is next placed on the crocks, the climber planted and the container filled with soil in the usual way. In order to ensure that the moss mixture is kept continually moist, a small flowerpot is inserted in the top end of the cylinder and this is kept topped up daily with water. The climber is trained up the cylinder and held in position by means of U-shaped pieces of wire inserted on the slant into the moss mixture (see Figure 3, page 37).

Chlorophytum capense 'Variegatum' (Spider Plant) is among the easiest to grow and most tolerant of house plants. It grows as a dense tuft of arching leaves, rather like grass, that are edged bright green with a stripe of cream through the centre. Its insignificant white flowers are produced on long, corn-coloured stalks, which stand above the plant. After flowering, small plantlets develop on them and these weigh them down, giving a pendulous or trailing effect and making the plant very effective for hanging baskets. The plant can be easily propagated by layering, i.e. by pinning these tiny tufts down in compost with a hairpin and cutting them off when they have rooted.

It prefers a bright position, but not direct sunlight. It grows best in a medium humid place at a temperature of 65°–

Figure 1

Figure 2

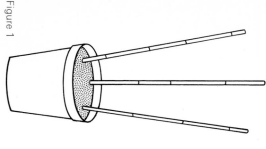

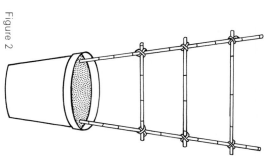

Two methods of supporting climbing house plants (page 33)

75°F (18°–24°C), with a drop of about 10°F at night. C. Chlorophytum capense 'Variegatum' should be kept reasonably moist and never allowed to dry out. Repotting into a slightly larger container annually is advantageous.

Cissus antarctica (Kangaroo Vine). This is a very easy-to-grow, tough, fast-growing, self-clinging climber, reaching, if permitted, a height of eight feet. It is excellent grown as a room divider. It has lovely, fresh green oval leaves, which are well veined. It is easily propagated by layering.

Although it does best in good light, out of strong sun, it may also do fairly well in sunless and more shady rooms. It is quite tolerant of lower temperatures and will thrive at a temperature level of 50°F (10°C). It enjoys a medium humid atmosphere. It should be well watered at intervals during the summer and between waterings be allowed to dry out almost completely. It needs very little water during the winter. The variety 'Russikivin' is recommended.

C. discolor has beautiful green, reddish-purple, mottled-white leaves. It is much less easy to grow than C. antarctica, and requires a much higher temperature and moist atmosphere to thrive. It has the disadvantage of tending to lose its leaves in

Hanging below the basket:
Cissus Discolor, above: Fittonia
Argyroneura (left)

Chlorophytum Comosum
Pictaratum (below)

Fittonia verschaffeltii (Snakeskin Plant) is a very beautiful trailer with smallish, heart-shaped, dark-green leaves, criss-crossed with a network of crimson veins. It is probably most suited to a bottle garden or a terrarium, but can be trained as a climber or trailer in a hanging basket. It is, however, fastidious regarding its conditions. It needs a warm room, with a temperature not lower than 60°F (15°C) in the winter; it must be shaded from direct sunlight; and it likes a fairly humid atmosphere. It only requires moderate watering, but it should not be allowed to dry out.

Hederas (True Ivies) are the most valuable of all climbing and trailing house plants and can be most effectively employed for all the functions of this type of plant. They can be planted in baskets, to grow over the edges of bowls, to climb supports of bamboo canes, and as room dividers. It is also becoming the vogue to grow indoors ivy standard plants, using fatshedera as root stock. Although it takes some time to achieve because, to be really attractive, the stem should be three to four feet tall, it is not difficult for a 'do-it-yourself' gardener to create his own ivy standard. This is done by first cutting back all the shoots from a fatshedera, except one which is growing more or

winter, but this can be avoided if given the right conditions. *C. striata* is very much more delicate than *C. antarctica* and *C. antarctica* needs more moisture, but it is useful because it is more dwarf in habit.

Ficus pumila (Creeping Fig) is a very attractive, small, hardy climbing or trailing plant, which has small, bright-green leaves, with their veins of a much darker hue. It is easy to grow. It produces aerial roots, which cling to a moss stick or, in fact, a rough surface such as a piece of bark, or the outside walls of a container. It is excellent for hanging baskets or for trailing over the edge of dishes. It is easily propagated by layering.

It is a particularly unusual plant because it prefers cool or average rooms. It loathes direct sun, revels in moist air and must be well watered and never allowed to dry out even in the winter. It is tolerant of gas and other fumes.

F. radicans 'Variegata' is very attractive for a hanging basket, but it is a different plant and must be kept in a very moist atmosphere. The temperature of its environment should never be lower than 50°F (10°C). Its rather beautiful, small green and white leaves make it worth persevering with.

less vertically, staking it and removing all but the top growth until it has reached the required height. The top of the plant is then cut off and a horizontal cut, half an inch deep, is made across the cross-section of the stem. Four cuttings of ivy, each about four inches long, are inserted into this and they are bound in with raffia or plastic tape.

Hedera helix (Common Ivy). Even this common ivy species, with its deep-green, shiny leaves, makes an excellent house plant. Some of its varieties and those of other species, with their bright colours, and differently shaped, smaller leaves, are even better.

Very useful varieties of the common ivy that are most suitable as house plants are:

H. helix 'Adam'. This has grey-green, variegated, perfectly shaped, tiny leaves, closely packed to the extent of overlapping on the stems. Care should be taken not to wet the centre of the plant, otherwise rotting is likely to occur.

H. helix 'Chicago' has small, dark-green leaves, often stained bronze-purple.

H. helix 'Cristata' is a distinctive form of ivy. It has pale-green leaves that are rather charmingly twisted and crinkled at the

edges. It has been likened to parsley, while others have called it 'Holly Ivy'. It likes to be kept drier than other varieties.

H. helix 'Glacier' is one of the most effective of the 'silver' ivies with its small, silvery-grey leaves with thin white margins. It is an excellent trailer.

H. helix 'Golden Jubilee'. Its leaves are small and golden, with a broad, dark-green margin, which makes it unusual.

H. helix 'Sagittifolia'. This variety has leaves that are five-lobed, the central one of which is large and triangular. They are small and dark green, and have slightly white veins.

H. helix 'Shamrock'. This variety has small, very dark-green leaves.

A hedera of another species, which is most popular as a house plant in these days, is *H. canariensis* 'Variegata', the Canary Island Ivy. It has large leaves, deep green in the middle, fading to silvery grey with a white margin.

All ivies are hardy, except that *H. canariensis* 'Variegata' should not be exposed to frost. They prefer a shady, fairly cool room, but they can be acclimatized to heat if the air is kept humid. During the winter the interesting colour of *H. canariensis* 'Variegata' can be preserved by putting it into a

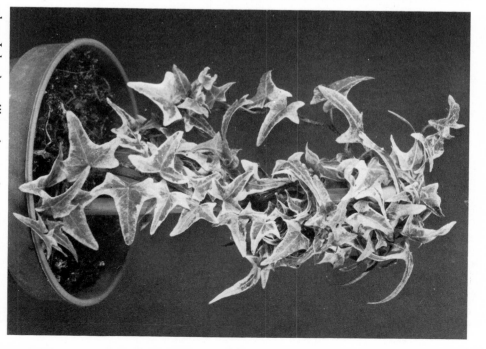

Hedera Helix Glacier (below left)

Hedera Helix Sagittifolia (below)

Hedera Canariensis (right)

A moss stick or totem pole (page 33)
Figure 3

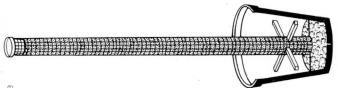

well-lit position. Ivies should be kept moist during the summer, but not over-watered. During the winter, the water supply should be considerably reduced. Hederas prefer to be grown in small pots.

Philodendrons. Probably this group contains some of the best-known foliage plants. It is difficult to find leaves of more beauty and with such variable and lovely shapes. These plants probably grow better in the conditions found in modern homes than any other house plants. Little harm comes to them if they are kept warm, if possible in a temperature of not less than 65°F (18°C), moderately moist, are allowed to dry out between waterings, and out of direct sunlight. They are not difficult to grow, but their beauty is so rewarding that it is worth while giving them just that little bit of extra care. While some are dwarf bush plants, many are climbers.

The most popular of the climbing philodendrons is no doubt *P. scandens*. It is certainly the easiest of all house plants for a beginner. It is an excellent plant for a dark room. Although it likes warm conditions, it will grow reasonably in a cool room. It is unaffected by gas and other fumes. It is primarily a climbing plant and throws out many aerial roots, and

is therefore ideal for climbing a moss stick. It can, nevertheless, be grown as a bushy plant if the leader is regularly pinched out. Because of its heart-shaped leaves, it is commonly called in England 'the Sweetheart Vine'; in America, it is known as 'the Bathroom Plant' which is a reflection of the living conditions it likes best. A very similar, but what appears to be a larger version of this plant, P. cordatum (oxycardium), 'the Totem Pole Philodendron', is popular in the United States.

There are other climbing philodendrons, some with similar characteristics, but none is quite so easy to grow or as accommodating as P. scandens. The most interesting of the others are:
P. bipennifolium which has grey-green foliage and aerial roots. It is fairly easy to grow.
P. elegans. This plant has charming divided foliage. It grows well in shade in an average room.
P. erubescens. Its arrow-shaped leaves have a rosy tinge when young, becoming dark green and purplish. It makes aerial roots. It is fairly easy to grow in average or warm rooms. It is a large plant.
P. laciniatum has medium-sized, dark leaves.

P. leichtlinii is an interesting slender climber with fantastic, evenly slashed, oval leaves, but it is difficult to grow, needing more heat and humidity than can be comfortably supplied in living-rooms.
P. melanochryson (andreanum) has small, dark-purple leaves with a velvet sheen. It grows aerial roots. It needs a warm position continuously. The soil should be kept fairly dry in winter.

Rhoicissus rhomboidea (Cissus rhombifolia, Grape Ivy). This climber, and trailer, if you wish, which has much the same glossy, green, veined foliage as Cissus antarctica, can be distinguished from it by the fact that its leaflets emerge from the stem in groups of three at one point, whereas in Cissus antarctica, they grow singly at intervals along the stalk. It enjoys a centrally-heated room, but it is quite tolerant of any average one. It likes good light, but not direct sunshine. It should be watered freely in the summer and moderately in the winter. It is easy to grow, quick-growing, easy to propagate by layering or by cuttings and is probably the most durable of all house plants.

Scindapsus aureus (Devil's Ivy) can quite excusably be mis-

Philodendron Scandens (left)

Scindapsus Aureus Marble Queen (below)

Hedera Helix Chicago (bottom left)

taken for a variegated philodendron. It does in fact need to be handled in much the same way as these plants. It has heart-shaped, green and yellow leaves. When grown vertically it needs to have the support of a moss stick (totem pole), so that its numerous aerial roots can absorb moisture. Although it is not so happy grown in this fashion, it is probably one of the best house plants to trail over the edge of a dish garden. It is not an easy plant, and does best in slight shade. When it is young the leaves tend to brown at the edges, but if well cared for, this shortcoming is overcome as it becomes established. Its cultivar, *S. aureus* 'Marble Queen', which has cream leaves flecked with green, is a somewhat slower grower, but has a beautiful form. *S. pictus* 'Argyraeus', which has silver-spotted leaves, is also very lovely.

Syngonium podophyllum (*Nephthytis*, Goose Foot). This most attractive plant, with its three-pronged, arrowhead-like, cream-tinted leaves, and many aerial roots, thrives most happily when climbing a moist moss stick. It grows pretty well in warm or average rooms, under normal household conditions. The pot should be allowed to dry out between waterings. Its near relative, *S. vellozianum*, grows satisfactorily

Tetrastigma voinierianum (Chestnut Vine, Lizard Plant). This derives its name from its dark-green, horsechestnut-shaped leaves, which can measure almost a foot across. It is a fairly large, quick-growing plant and requires plenty of room, which makes it very suitable for large offices, vestibules and shops. It likes good, even light, but not direct sunlight, a large pot, to be well watered in the summer, with infrequent watering in the winter, to be fed regularly with liquid manure in the summer, moist air and warmth.

Tradescantia fluminensis (Wandering Jew, Travelling Sailor, Wandering Plant) is the best known of this species. There are both yellow and white variegated forms as well as green. If the former revert to green, such shoots should be cut off immediately. They are easy to grow in average and warm rooms if given plenty of water in the summer and considerably less in the winter, and good light. They will grow in shade, but they lose a good deal of their beautiful colour. Most tradescantias become straggly and defoliated with age,

particularly in a dry atmosphere. They are so easily propagated from cuttings that this can be readily overcome by replacing them from time to time. They are most useful house plants for wall brackets, hanging baskets, trailing over the edge of containers and in bottle gardens. Attractive varieties of *T. fluminensis* are 'Variegata' (white stripes on green leaves) and 'Aurea' with yellow stripes. *T. albiflora*, which has leaves with green, pink, and white markings, and its cultivar, 'Tricolor' are also very lovely. A little more difficult to grow is the species, *T. blossfeldiana*, which has green, glossy leaves that are purple underneath.

Zebrina pendula (formerly *Tradescantia zebrina*), which is closely related to the tradescantias, is a very beautiful, easily grown plant, that can be used for much the same purposes. The upper surfaces of its leaves are silvery, edged green, with a purple centre stripe and bright purple on their undersides, which colours are appreciably enhanced if the plant is kept a little on the dry side. *Z. purpusii* has dark-mauve, rather large leaves.

Rhoicissus Rhomboidea
(below left)

Scindapsus Aureus Devil's Ivy
(below right)

Hedera Helix Prostata (bottom
left)

Philodendron Bipennifolium
(bottom right)

42

Begonia Rex (right)

Aglaonema Treubii (below left)

Begonia Masoniana in flower (below right)

Cryptanthus Bivittatus (bottom left)

Begonia Masoniana (bottom right)

Bushy and Upright Foliage Plants

Bushy foliage house plants have very beautiful leaves and can be put to many attractive uses in modern homes, both as individual specimens and in arrangements. In the ensuing paragraphs, the more popular ones are discussed in detail.

Acorus gramineus 'Variegatus' is a very attractive, easy-to-grow, grass-like plant, that grows upright to a height of about six inches. Its leaves are striped green and cream along their length. It needs light and a fairly cool position. Being a water-side plant, it cannot be kept too wet. It is an excellent subject for bottle and dish gardens.

Aglaonema commutatum (Chinese Evergreen). This is not easy to grow. To be successful, it should be maintained at a temperature of $60°–70°F$ ($15°–21°C$), with no winter fluctuations. It likes shade and moisture and dislikes fumes. It should be watered well and given liquid manure during summer, with only a little watering during the winter. It appreciates being sprayed with clean water in hot and dry weather. With its nine-inch long, dark-green leaves that are blotched white, it is an attractive plant. So is its compact cultivar 'Silver Queen' which has silver-grey leaves.

Aralia elegantissima, Dizygotheca elegantissima (Finger Aralia). Its unusual finger-like, long narrow leaves, not more than half an inch wide, make this a most graceful house plant. They are deeply serrated and spread out in a flat plane at the end of its dark-green, mottled stalks. The young foliage is of a reddish brown, becoming almost black with age. When young and about eighteen inches tall, it is excellent for mixed groups, but a tall, mature specimen adds much to the décor of any room.

It is not easy to grow and requires warmth ($60°F$, $15°C$) and moisture, particularly during winter, and good light. Draughts and fluctuations in temperature must be avoided. It should not at any time be over-watered.

Araucaria excelsa (Norfolk Island Pine). Being related to the monkey-puzzle tree, this house plant grows in its habitat to a height of 100–150 feet, but kept in a small pot, it becomes dwarfed. It has very beautiful layers of emerald-green needles, which makes it an excellent permanent substitute for a Christmas tree. In a cool, light or shady room, it will grow slowly for a long time if it is kept moist. Should the

needles begin to fall, the pot should be stood on a pebble tray (see page 132–3).

Aspidistra lurida, Aspidistra elatior (Cast Iron Plant, Parlour Palm). As its first common name suggests, this plant is the hardiest of all foliage house plants, withstanding with equanimity gas, deep shade, neglect, heat, dust, dryness of air and soil, but not bright sunshine. Any care, however, brings its rewards. All it asks for is to be kept moist, given moderate humidity and reasonable warmth. It likes having its leaves sponged occasionally and to be given spells out of doors in the summer rain. The leaves of both the dark-green and variegated varieties are prized by flower arrangers.

Begonias. The growing conditions that are liked by begonias are given on page 65. Probably the most decorative of all begonias, which is grown for the beauty of its foliage, is *Begonia rex.* The colour of its large, approximately triangular leaves covers a wide range. It includes silver to dark green and pink to the darkest purple. The patterns on the leaves are almost indescribable and are composed of dots, stripes and splashes of numerous contrasting colours with bands on their edges and the path of their veins. Superimposed on all this glamour is an exquisite metallic sheen. Another low-growing, bushy, foliage begonia is *B. masoniana*, which, because of the purplish-brown Iron Cross marked on the medium-green background of each of its leaves is commonly known as the 'Iron Cross Begonia'. It grows into an extremely distinctive plant.

Both species are indeed superb and put up the most glorious display when planted either as specimens or in groupings, either in dishes or bottle gardens.

Caladium candidum. With their fragile-looking, delightfully shaped, variously coloured leaves, caladiums are among the most beautiful of foliage plants. They are, however, among the most difficult to grow. So much so that they are worth treating as flowering pot plants, because they can usually only survive the winter in a heated greenhouse.

C. candidum, which is the most popular, has almost transparent, snowy-green leaves that are veined a delicate green. Attractive varieties are 'Mary Moir', with its pale-green leaves, heavily veined bottle green, with maroon flecks, 'Mrs F. M. Joyner' whose leaves are rose centred with edges of

Codiaeum Variegatum Croton (below left)

Cryptanthus Bromelioides Tricolor (below right)

dark green and 'Frieda Hemple', brilliant carmine with an avocado-pear green margin.

Calathea mackoyana (Peacock Plant). This is the best known of the very decorative calatheas, which, having markings rather similar to the Marantas, are sometimes offered as such. It has very lovely silvery-green leaves with veins of dark green and edged with medium green. It is excellent for a bottle garden. As it is not easy to grow, it is often better to regard it as expendable. All calatheas need to be kept very warm, in the shade and in a moist atmosphere. They should be well watered during the summer, with considerably less in the winter. Possibly easier to grow, but less colourful are *C. insignis*, *C. ornata sanderiana* and *C. louisae*.

Codiaeum variegatum pictum (South Sea Laurel). This vertical-growing, single-stemmed plant and its varieties are commonly known as crotons. Their leaves are deeply veined, varying in shape, sometimes straight, other times twisted and variously patterned with orange, yellow, red, green and black. Crotons are difficult to acclimatize and need to be in a continuously centrally-heated, humid room, free from draughts and out of bright sunshine.

C. variegatum pictum is an excellent plant for a bottle garden. Its very colourful cultivars are red and crimson *chelsoni*, the 'Blood Red Croton', Pennick, orange-pink *reidii*, *thompsonii*, which is gold, chocolate and crimson and green, crimson and magenta *williamsii*. *C. ostenzee* is a slow grower with dainty narrow, variegated yellow and green leaves.

As crotons become older, they often lose their lower leaves. This can be remedied by air-layering (see page 50).

Cordyline terminalis (Flaming Dragon Tree). There is some confusion about the botanical classification of this plant. It is additionally known as *Dracaena baptistii*, *D. terminalis*, *D. indivisa* and is often sold by florists as a 'Dracaena'. Whatever it is called, however, it has pink, cerise, or cream, oval young leaves, that eventually become mainly green and red with splashings and margins of these brighter colours. Its palm-like leaves are much sought after by flower arrangers. It is relatively easy to grow in an average light room. If the lower leaves fall as it grows older, this can be remedied by air-layering (see page 50).

Cryptanthus (Starfish Plant, Star Plant and, because its leaves change colour on moving in and out of the sun, Chameleon).

Group of Cryptanthus, from the back clockwise. C. Zonatus. C. Aucalis. C. Bivittatus

They are all low-growing bromeliads, that are easy to grow, provided they are given good light and not too much water. The two most common species are *C. bivittatus* with nine-inch long, evergreen leaves, with sharply toothed edges and two yellow bands running along their length and *C. zonatus*, that has alternative green and silvery-grey bands across its leaves of similar length, which are whitish underneath. Also there are *C. tricolor*, with cream stripes diffused with pink, and mottled-leaved *C. fosteriana*.

Ctenanthe lubbersiana. This plant has very attractive, narrow leaves about eight inches long, which have their undersides pale green with their upper surface a deep green variegated with yellow. In bright sunshine, which it dislikes, the edges of its leaves roll up. It needs a shady, warm and moist position for success, and is good in a bottle garden.

Cyperus alternifolius. Being a swamp lover, it cannot be over-watered. It is easy to grow and will thrive in an unheated area. It has grass-like leaves emanating from its base, from which it also produces tall flowering stems which are domi-nated by crowns of shorter leaves, giving the appearance of an umbrella. Hence its common name 'Umbrella Plant'.

Dieffenbachia picta (Dumb Cane, Mother-in-Law Plant). Most dieffenbachias are tall, handsome plants with prominently marked leaves. They all need a fairly high and constant temperature and, provided good humidity is present, they do well in a centrally-heated room. Although deep shade might reduce their variegation, they do better in a shady position. They appear to be unaffected by gas fumes. They need well watering in the summer, with considerable reduc-tion in winter. Their large leaves should be sprayed with water every ten days. Their sap is poisonous, and children and pets should not have access to them.

D. picta has dark-green, pointed oblong leaves, covered with white and pale-green spots. Its cultivar 'Rudolph Roehrs' is mottled pale and dark green. *D. exotica* (*arvida*) has large, irregular markings of creamy white and *D. amoena* with its white feathering on immense, glossy, green leaves can be a valuable asset in any décor.

If they lose their lower leaves, air-layering (see page 50) can put this right.

Dracaena (Dragon Plant). All dracaenas are very lovely, com-paratively tall, slow-growing, foliage plants. Most species

Cryptanthus Zonatus Brunei (right)

Cryptanthus Zonatus (below left)

Dieffenbachia Picta (below right)

Ctenanthe Oppenheimiana Tricolor (bottom left)

Cordyline Terminalis (bottom right)

46

have long, firm, silky, long-lasting, pointed leaves, that are variously striped. Most of them shed their lower leaves as they grow taller, but this is not to their disadvantage. While they grow under average conditions, they are at their best in centrally-heated rooms, in which the temperature is never lower than 55°F (13°C) and the humidity is reasonably low. They need to be well watered in the summer, but this must be reduced during winter. Generally dracaenas do well in both bright and medium light, but indirect sunlight is beneficial to the variegated types. There are two more dwarf dracaenas, which are very attractive in the house:

D. godseffiana, which is one of the shorter growing types, has dark-green leaves with pale-yellow spots.

D. sanderi (*D. sanderiana*), which is smaller than most, is very attractive with its grey-green leaves, bordered with a white band. It thrives in semi-shade. It is a good plant for dish and bottle gardens.

Among the larger types are *D. deremensis* 'Warnecki', which has grey-green leaves with two silver stripes and *D. deremensis* 'Bausei', with its dark-green leaves with a broad central stripe of white, growing from silvery coloured stems. Others

are *D. fragrans*, which has broad, strap-shaped leaves with a gold band down their centres, *D. marginata*, which is perhaps a little easier to grow than the rest and has dull red-margined leaves and, finally, *D.* 'Firebrand' which is unusual but very lovely, with its narrow pink and red leaves.

Fatshedera lizei (Fat-headed Lizzie, Ivy Tree). This plant, which is a cross between the fatsia and ivy, has the characteristics of both its parents. It will grow eight feet tall or more, but it can be kept bushy by pinching out the leader. Its leaves, which have the texture and colour of the fatsia, have the shape of the ivy. It is easy to grow in cold and average rooms, particularly as it needs no winter heat. It should be well watered in the summer, but not excessively so, because this tends to brown the leaf edges. Direct sunlight tends to make its leaves wilt.

Fatsia japonica (Aralia, Castor Oil Plant, Fig Leaf Palm). This large-growing plant, which is happy in cold and average rooms, is excellent for an entrance hall. In average size rooms, it can be kept bushy by topping it in the spring. It is a very valuable accent plant, with its large, glossy green, round leaves, which have up to seven or nine blunt points.

Ficus (Ornamental Fig). Some of the climbers of this genera have already been described on page 35. There is little doubt that ficus are the most popular among the house plants. This is because of the dramatic effect that they can impart to the décor of modern rooms.

F. benjamina (Weeping Fig, Willow Fig) has the most fascinating ovate leaves, that quite abruptly terminate in a sharp point, closely clothing its graceful, drooping branches. It is not easy to grow, needing a well-lit, warm room, in which the temperature never falls below 50°F (10°C). It must not be over-watered, particularly in the winter when it partially rests and may lose some leaves. If it becomes too dry, however, it wilts.

F. elastica 'Decora' (India-Rubber Plant). This is probably the best known and easiest to grow ficus that has taken the place of the Victorian aspidistra in modern living. Being hardy, it adapts itself to both warm and cold conditions, but it prefers to be in a room in which the temperature never fluctuates or falls below 50°F (10°C) in the winter, and there is not too much sunshine. It appreciates generous summer watering and liquid feeding, with less watering in the winter.

Dieffenbachia Exotica (below left)

Dracaena Marginata (below right)

Cyperus Alternifolius Variegata (bottom right)

Maranta Massangeana Erythrophylla

It enjoys having its leaves washed frequently in luke-warm water. It is happier when planted in a small pot.

It grows dignified, large, shiny, leathery, dark-green leaves, that first appear clothed in a red sheath, almost like a flower. Although it grows six to eight feet tall, it can be kept smaller by being cut back in the spring. Its tall growth and tolerance to cooler conditions make it an excellent specimen for shops, hotels and offices, in which it is in full harmony with any décor. Although rather more difficult to grow, its variegated counterpart, *F. elastica* 'Tricolor' with its leaves of pink, silvery-grey, cream and green is a very beautiful house plant.

Air-layering. F. elastica 'Decora', in common with cordyline, dracaena, dieffenbachia and fatshedera (see pages 44–7), loses its lower leaves as it matures. As mentioned previously, this can be overcome by air-layering. To do this, a narrow ring is cut in the bark at a point about twelve inches below the tip of the plant. This is moistened with water and hormone rooting compound is applied to it with a camel-hair brush. It is then covered with a sizeable handful of sphagnum moss, which is bound into position with raffia and covered completely with a small sheet of polythene, which is affixed to the stem with cellophane tape. When the roots can be seen through the polythene, the stem is cut below the bundle of moss and the new plant is potted. The remaining stem on the old plant is cut down to soil level. With watering and feeding, new shoots will soon appear (see Figures 4, 5, page 54).

F. lyrata, F. pandurata (Fiddle-leaved Fig, Fiddle Leaf'). The leathery leaves of this large, handsome house plant, which

Fatsia Japonica (below)

Ficus Elastica Decora; the popular india-rubber plant (right)

Monstera Deliciosa Borsigiana (bottom right)

Grevillea Robusta (left)

Ficus Benjamina (bottom left)

Ficus Elastica Decora (bottom right)

eventually grow eighteen inches long, are in the shape of a violin. They are strikingly marked with cream-coloured veins. Although a little more difficult to grow, it reacts to much the same handling as *F. elastica* 'Decora'. It is superb in a spacious hall.

F. schryveriana. The leaves of this hardy ficus which are green and yellow, are smaller than those of *F. elastica* 'Decora'.

Fittonia argyroneura (Snakeskin Plant) is a low-growing plant that is difficult to grow because of its heavy demand for warmth and humidity. It is, nevertheless, very attractive with its dark-green leaves, heavily veined with silver. *F. verschaffeltii* has pinkish-red veins on very dark leaves. Of the two, it is the easier to keep outside a bottle garden.

Grevillea robusta (Australian Wattle, Silk Oak). This beautiful evergreen shrub has silvery, finely divided foliage. It is easy to grow. It must not be allowed to dry out, because otherwise its leaves drop. It ultimately grows very tall.

Gynura sarmentosa. This delightful plant grows either upright or as a trailer. It is a great joy with its velvety, purple foliage. Its rather unattractive, ill-smelling, orange flowers are better removed. It likes central heating, good lighting and being

Nidularium Fulgens (below)

An attractive variety of
Dieffenbachia (right)

allowed to dry out between waterings. Its cuttings root very easily.

Helxine soleirolii (Mind Your Own Business, Baby's Tears). This rather invasive, carpeting plant is very easy to grow, but it should be used with discrimination. Its bright-green, rounded foliage looks beautiful if it is allowed to grow alone in a shallow pan. It is a water lover, and best grown with its pot standing in a saucer of water. It grows in deep shade, but ideally it should have a moist, cool, partially shady position. It abhors gas fumes.

Laurus nobilis (Bay Tree). This evergreen, the leaves of which are prized by cooks, makes an excellent and useful indoor shrub. It will succeed in any normal soil, but it is a lover of full sun. Its size can be kept under control by careful trimming or by picking the leaves for drying for storage.

Maranta. The plants in this group are not easy to grow because they need warmth, shade, root moisture and humidity. They are excellent for bottle gardens and terrariums because of their very ornamental foliage. Similarly, they can give a dramatic effect to the simplest dish garden.

Maranta leuconeura 'Kerchoveana' (Prayer Plant, Husband and Wife). Its first common name comes from its habit of closing up its leaves at sundown. It is a delightful bushy plant with prominent purple-maroon blotches on either side of its centre veins.

M. leuconeura 'Erythrophylla' (Tricolor) is attractive with its bright-green leaves with red and brown markings.

M. picturata has light-grey leaves with dark-green edges and maroon underneath. It is difficult to grow.

Monstera deliciosa 'Borsigiana' is a giant, handsome foliage plant that fortunately grows fairly slowly in a small pot; it can also be kept down in height by cutting out its top periodically. Its enormous dark-green leaves are slashed and perforated in an almost startling fashion. Its new leaves, which are produced from a long cone-shaped bud attached to the stem of an old one, are very glossy and delicate green in colour. It produces abundant, long aerial roots, which can beneficially be tied together and inserted in the soil in its pot. Another feature is that in time it produces a flower, followed by a delicious fruit with an elusive flavour between that of pineapple and banana. For this reason, the Australians call it the 'Fruit Salad Plant'.

Although it will adapt itself to cooler conditions, it likes warmth, good humidity, plenty of water and feeding during summer. The soil should be allowed to become fairly dry between waterings. It has no objection to smoke or gas fumes.

Neoregelias are bromeliads (pineapple family). They have striking, colourful foliage, particularly in their cup-like centres which, during the growing season, should be kept filled with tepid water, preferably rainwater. They have insignificant flowers that grow in these centres. When they fade they should be removed with tweezers and the cups washed out because otherwise they smell unpleasantly. Neoregelias need well-lit quarters and a temperature that never falls below 50°F (10°C).

Neoregelia carolinae has a brilliant vermilion foliage centre.

N. carolinae 'Tricolor' has green leaves with lengthwise-running, pinky-cream stripes and a pinky-red centre.

N. marechali is particularly attractive. It has broad, strap-like, bright-green leaves with spiny edges and a bright-red centre.

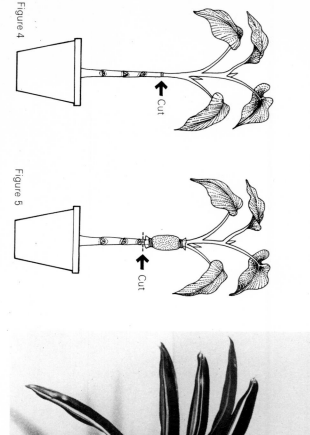

Figure 4

Figure 5

Cut

Cut

Air layering a plant that has lost its lower leaves (page 50)

Neoregelia Carolinae Tricolor (bottom right)

Maranta Leuconeura
Kerchoveana

Nidularium fulgens (Bird's Nest Bromeliad) is generally easy to grow. It prefers a minimum temperature of 50°F (10°C), and should not be kept too wet, even in the summer, but its central nest of scarlet leaves should be kept filled with water after its whitish lilac-coloured flowers have faded. It has gorgeous, twelve-inch long and two-inch broad, dark-green leaves with up to ten short scarlet ones in the centre.

Pandanus veitchii (Screw Pine). This palm-like plant, which has long and narrow leaves, with serrated edges like those of a pineapple, is difficult to grow, needing constant warmth, a temperature never below 55°F (13°C) and a moist atmosphere. It does best in central heating. It needs to be well watered during the summer, but it should be allowed to become fairly dry between waterings. It likes a small pot. *Peperomias*. These are moderate or small plants with very lovely leaves and flowers, sometimes carried high on colourful stalks, which together make the plants extraordinarily decorative.

They all require warmth, humidity, some shade and, as they have small roots, to be grown in small well-drained pots. At no time should they be excessively watered and should be

kept rather drier in winter than is usual for plants kept under warm conditions. They are very suitable for bottle gardens. *P. caperata* is among the best known. It has dark-green, corrugated leaves on pink stems and curious, cream flowers, like shepherds' crooks, borne on light-brown stalks. It will grow in deep shade.

P. hederifolia is similar to, but rather larger than, *P. caperata*. Its glossy leaves are less crinkled and metallic grey-green in colour. It is a little more tender.

P. magnoliaefolia (*P. obtusifolia* 'Variegata') is a tough, but slower-growing, shrubby plant, which has brilliant cream and green leaves, borne on short, branching, reddish stems. The most beautiful of all is *P. sandersii* (*P. argyreia*), called the Watermelon Peperomia, because of the shape of leaves, which are dark green patterned with crescents of silver. It forms a very lovely clump.

Philodendrons. The culture of these beautiful foliage plants has been discussed on pages 35, 37. In addition to the climbers and trailers dealt with there, there are several lovely bushy species that are very valuable for decoration, see page 59. Although it requires plenty of room for dis-

Stephanotis Floribunda
(left)

Passiflora John Innes
(right)

Philodendron Leichtlinii (top left)

Pilea Microphylla (top right)

Fittonia Argyroneura (middle left)

Dracaena Deremensis Warnecki (middle right)

Tolmiea Menziesii (bottom left)

Nidularium Abolineata (bottom right)

Pilea Cadierei Nana (below left)

Pilea Mollis (below right)

play, it is not difficult to grow. The long fleshy roots that emerge from its growing point should be trained back into the soil.

P. 'Burgundy' is very tolerant. It benefits very much from the support of a moist moss stick into which its aerial roots can penetrate. It assumes a rich hue from the reflection of the colour of its deep, wine-red stem in its superb two-foot long leaves.

P. dubium is slow growing and never gets out of hand.

P. pertusum is like a smaller version of *Monstera deliciosa* and is often referred to as such.

P. selloum. This very striking, sturdy, slow-growing philodendron has its very large leaves cut into strips half-way to the midrib. As they fall, they leave white scars on the stem, which add to its attractiveness. It is particularly resistant to cold and will stand freezing temperatures.

P. wendlandi is tolerant of extremes of temperature and humidity. It is compact and has long narrow leaves.

Pilea cadierei (Aluminium Plant, Friendship Plant) is a very decorative, small, bushy plant with pointed oval leaves that are dark green with broken aluminium stripes. It is easy to

grow in an average or warm room, and is excellent for growing in a bottle garden and as a low component of a dish garden. It dislikes strong sunshine and likes plenty of water and liquid manure during the summer. There is a dwarf version, *P. cadierei 'Nana'.*

P. muscosa (microphylla) (Artillery Plant, Gunpowder Plant, Pistol Plant) is quite unlike *cadierei* with its minute, light-green, moss-like foliage, but it likes much the same environment. It is easy to grow.

Sansevieria trifasciata 'Laurentii' (Mother-in-Law's Tongue, Bayonet Plant, Snake Plant). This very decorative, but rather vicious-looking plant, is easy to grow. It loves sunshine, but does not mind shade; it is adaptable to high and low temperatures, but at the latter it should be kept fairly dry. It should be allowed to dry out between waterings. It has narrow, fleshy, pointed, slightly twisted leaves, edged with yellow and banded alternatively with light and dark green.

Saxifraga sarmentosa, S. stolonifera (Mother of Thousands) is a low-growing, hardy plant, that likes a cool room and dislikes sunshine. It should be grown in a small pot. Its leaves are particularly decorative and are dark green with cream-

Peperomia Magnoliaefolia
(below)

Tolmiea Menziesii (right)

Sanseviera Trifasciata Laurentii
(bottom left)

Peperomia Caperata (bottom
right)

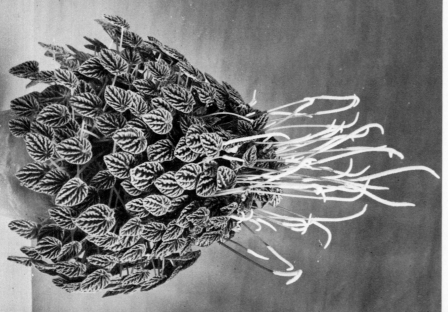

coloured veins, with their undersides purplish red. It is easily propagated by layering.

Schefflera actinophylla (Umbrella Tree) is a delightful foliage plant with glossy, green, long pointed leaves in groups of three or five at the top of a stalk, like the segments of an umbrella. It flourishes in almost any room, even in a dry atmosphere. It grows fairly quickly and eventually makes a large plant.

Setcreasea purpurea (Purple Heart) is a very attractive, rich purple, rather straggly, foliage plant. It is a quick grower that is easy to grow. Sunshine intensifies its colour. It likes a lot of water unless it is kept in a cool place.

Stenocarpus sinuatus is another easy-to-grow, nearly hardy plant, that is suitable for cold and average rooms, which are well lit. It does not like direct sunshine. It is very decorative, with light-green, glossy leaves that have a slight wave. The young leaves have three lobes, but they increase in number with age. With its leaves growing to six inches long, it can ultimately become large.

Tolmiea menziesii (Pick-a-back Plant, Piggyback Plant) is an easy-to-grow, simple plant, that grows in cold and average rooms. It likes shade and plenty of water and regular feeding during the summer, with reduced watering in the winter. It freely grows plantlets that can be cut off and potted.

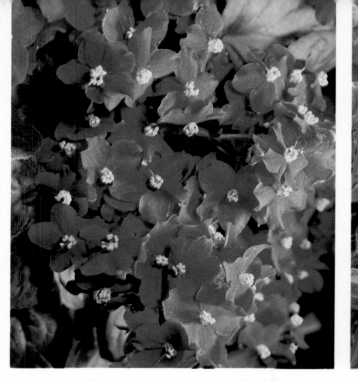

64

Aphelandra Squarrosa Daniae (right)

Passiflora Caerulea (below left)

Clivia Miniata (below right)

Saintpaulia Rochford Pamela (bottom left)

Citrus Mitis (bottom right)

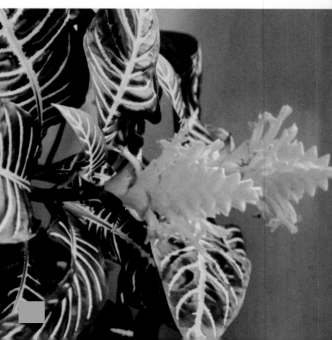

Flowering House Plants

Like foliage house plants, the foliage of flowering house plants remains alive and attractive throughout the year, but flowering house plants in addition can be expected to flower under room conditions, provided that their requirements are adequately met. Flowering house plants usually bloom better when the size of their pot is restricted. As in the case of the foliage plants, they can be divided into two categories, viz. climbers and trailers, and bushy plants.

Climbing and Trailing Flowering House Plants

Aeschyanthus speciosus is a beautiful plant for indoor decoration. It has long stems bearing lovely fleshy, deep-green, narrow leaves and clusters of orange, tubular, fragrant flowers at their extremities. It is either grown in hanging baskets or as a climber on supports in pots.

It should be planted in a rich mixture of sifted leaf-mould and a little sphagnum moss and should be repotted each year. It likes good drainage. It should be well watered in the summer and kept reasonably dry during winter at a temperature of about 50°F (10°C). It should not be allowed to flower during its first season.

Begonias generally like a well-lit place, far away from gas fumes. They are best when their pot is surrounded by damp peat (see page 132–3). They need to be watered well in the growing season and kept comparatively dry when they are resting. The leaves should on no account be wetted. In winter, a temperature of 50°–55°F (10°–13°C) should always be maintained. The most recommended climbing species is *Begonia glaucophylla*, which has shiny, pointed, greyish-green leaves, which make a very lovely foil for its brick-red flowers in pendulous clusters, which appear in spring and summer. It is also excellent for hanging baskets. It does not like hot rooms.

B. glabra is another suitable climbing begonia; it has small white flowers.

Columnea banksii needs a warm room in which the winter temperature does not fall below 55°F (13°C). It needs plenty of water during the growing period, but the soil should not be kept continuously saturated. The atmosphere should be kept humid by surrounding its pot with damp peat (see page 132–3). It likes a well-lit place out of direct sunlight. Its massed, reddish-orange flowers are three inches long and an inch and a half wide, and tubular in shape. It is a difficult plant to grow, but perseverance aimed at getting the right conditions is richly rewarded.

Another glorious columnea is *C. gloriosa* 'Purpurea', which has the most exotic-looking, orange flowers and small, dark-purple, hairy leaves.

Hoya carnosa (Wax Plant, Porcelain Flower) is an easy-to-grow plant with glossy, fleshy leaves and clusters of pale-pink, sweetly scented flowers that appear in summer. To be successful, it must have warmth and plenty of water when in flower. When the plant is growing it needs to be watered freely and given an occasional feed of liquid manure. When the plant is at the flower-bud stage, feeding should be stopped and watering reduced very considerably. It can stand cold conditions in the winter, but it flowers best in the shade where it is warm. There is a very beautiful variegated variety, *H. carnosa* 'Variegata', which has cream and green leaves. Another attractive species is *H. australis*, which has pink, flushed, white, honeysuckle-scented flowers.

Jasmine. There are two equally beautiful jasmines that will flower in the house, particularly if they are kept in an atmosphere that is warm, not less than 45°F (7o°C) in the winter, and fairly moist and in a sunny place. Under these conditions both are evergreen. Their size can be kept under control by stopping the shoots during the growing season. The first of these is *Jasminum polyanthum*, which resembles the white garden jasmine. It has white, highly perfumed flowers, pink on the outside, and dark-green leaves. The other is *J. primulinum*, which blooms in spring or earlier, giving bright-yellow, semi-double flowers that are often an inch in diameter.

Passiflora caerulea (The Passion Flower) is a quick-growing, hardy climber. Blue is the more common, but *P. caerulea* 'Constance Elliott' is a very delightful white variety. A sunny position is needed. It should be given plenty of water during the summer and receive an occasional feed. The temperature should not fall below 50°F (10°C) in the winter. It dislikes coal and gas fires. Keep under control by pruning hard in early spring.

Stephanotis floribunda (Madagascar Jasmine) is an exotic-looking, highly perfumed, vigorous climber. It has white, waxy flowers. It has evergreen leaves, that are about three inches long and make an attractive foil to the blooms. It should be grown in a moist atmosphere and in a pot with good drainage surrounded with damp peat. It likes good light and warmth, with the winter temperature not falling below 55°F (13°C).

Bushy and Upright Growers

Anthurium scherzerianum (Flamingo Plant, Painter's Palette) is an impressive house plant. It is a difficult one because it needs to be kept in a centrally-heated room, in which there are no temperature changes. A constant temperature of 60°F (15°C) is ideal. It requires to be planted in a well-drained pot, surrounded by moist peat so that the atmosphere is moist, and to be given plenty of water. In the winter the peat should be reduced, but the plant must not be allowed to dry out. Frequent spraying with tepid water is an advantage. It should be placed in a well-lit place.

A. scherzerianum is a most colourful plant and is an asset to any interior decoration scheme. It has long, slender, shiny, lanceolate leaves, but its crowning glory is its wonderful wax-

like, flamboyant, scarlet flowers, which grow on tall red stems and are composed of a spathe about two to three inches long and the same width, and a spirally-twisted orange-red spadix. The combination of these gives the plant an unusual, but most attractive, appearance.

Aechmeas (Urn Plant). These plants, which are members of the pineapple family, are characterized by the large strap-like leaves that form a vase-like rosette at their base. If kept in comparatively small pots, they do well in most rooms and are adaptable to cooler and warmer conditions provided they are given good light and kept relatively dry in the winter. Even in summer they should not be watered too heavily, but their central part should be kept filled, if possible, with rain-water. The varieties most frequently seen are *Aechmea fulgens*, which has olive-green leaves, with a base of reddish purple and produces small blue-petalled flowers that grow from a red calyx, and *A. fasciata* (*A. rhodacyanea*), which has a rosette of leaves, striped in bands of grey and green, with small pink flowers growing from pink bracts. In both cases the flowers soon die, but the calyxes and bracts remain colourful for a long time. Both plants are not tall, but can be more than two

Hoya Bella (below left)

Hoya Carnosa (below)

Aechmea Rhodocyanea (right)

Aechmea Fasciata (below)

Aphelandra Chamissioniana in flower (bottom)

feet across and so need plenty of space.

Aphelandra squarrosa 'Louisae' (Zebra Plant) is another rather difficult, but very showy plant, which is well worth persevering with. It has been found that younger plants are more adaptable to house conditions than larger ones. It needs to be in a well-lit, but not sunlit, spot in which there is always moist and warm air. Its winter temperature should never be lower than 55°F (13°C). Its soil should be kept constantly moist in the summer, but not soggy, and on the dry side in the winter. Spraying the foliage is very advantageous.

It is a beautiful plant with ten-inch long, pointed, very dark-green leaves, of which the veins are boldly delineated in pale cream. Its beauty is further enhanced by its large yellow flowers, which should be removed after they fade. Very beautiful varieties are 'Brockfield' and 'Silver Beauty'.

Begonias. Among the more bushy types of begonias that flower well are *Begonia maculata*, which has very decorative, large, medium-green leaves, that are brightly spotted with silver. It produces pendulous bunches of bright-pink flowers for a long period at almost any time of the year. A winter-blooming begonia is *B. manicata*, which has erect flowering stems that bear small rose-pink flowers. The Christmas begonia (*Gloire de Lorraine* begonia), *B. cheimantha*, which gives a dense mass of bright-red or pink blooms in the winter, is usually discarded after flowering, but given a warm, light, humid position, with moderate watering, it can be made more permanent. The small fibrous-rooted begonia, *B. semperflorens* and its many varieties make quite excellent house plants, particularly if two cultivars of different colour are planted in the same small pot. They like a sunny window-sill.

Beloperone guttata (Shrimp Plant) is an easy-to-grow plant, which has fascinating, rather unusual, shrimp-pink flowers and bracts, that combined are reminiscent of shrimps in shape, growing at the end of arching stems laden with medium-green leaves. It needs a sunny position, plenty of water and regular feeding in spring and summer, with an occasional spraying when the weather is hot. It should be kept dryish and cool in the winter. To keep in shape and bushy, the plant should be pruned in spring.

Billbergia. These bromeliads are very widely grown because they are easy to grow and most rewarding. They tolerate cool winter conditions, dry air and, to a certain extent, gas fumes. They should, however, be put into a place with good light, and warmth encourages flowering. They should not be over-watered, but some liquid feeding while they are growing is certainly acceptable.

Billbergia nutans is almost hardy. It has narrow, twelve-inch long, evergreen leaves. It produces tall flowering stalks, which are surmounted by unusual, but picturesque nodding, transient, yellowish-green, violet-blue bordered flowers, that are accompanied by a pink bract, which persists five or six

Aechmea Orlandiana (left)

Aphelandra Squarrosa Brockfield (below)

Aphelandra Squarrosa Louisae (bottom left)

Aphelandra Squarrosa Louisae in full flower (bottom right)

days after the blooms fade.

B. undii, which is possibly more attractive, has boat-shaped, rosy-red bracts and flowers that are suffused with reddish-purple and greenish-yellow.

Callistemon citrinus (Bottle Brush Plant), which hails from Australia, is a beautiful evergreen shrub. The variety 'Splendens' has brilliant scarlet flowers, with very colourful, long stamens, over a long period. It grows in a cool room. It should be top dressed, because it grows best when somewhat pot-bound.

Campanula isophylla is sometimes classed as a trailer, because of its prostrate habit, which enables it to hang over the edge of a pot. Irrespective of whether they are white or blue, its one-inch across, star-shaped flowers, in which it is engulfed during the summer, are very charming. It grows best in a well-lit, cool and airy room. It should be fed and given plenty of water while growing, but kept rather dry in the winter. If it is dead-headed regularly, it will remain in flower over a long period.

Citrus mitis (Calamondin Orange) is an unusual house plant in that it often bears flowers and fruit simultaneously. It has white, sweet-scented blooms, followed by inedible, small oranges. It, together with other orange species, is not difficult to grow. Most of all it needs plenty of sunshine. It benefits from ample water and regular feeding during the summer, with drier winter conditions. The temperature in winter should not be less than 50°F (10°C), but it can stand in the open from June until it becomes cold.

Clivia miniata (Kafir Lily) is a spectacular, easy-to-grow house plant, with its strap-shaped, dark-green leaves and its dominating heads of orange flowers, that are produced in the spring. It is claimed to be as tough and as long-lasting as the aspidistra. It should be kept dry and at a temperature above 45°–50°F (7°–10°C) in the winter, but it likes good watering, being sprayed and occasional feeding during the summer months. It should be put in a well-lit room, but away from direct sunlight. As it blooms best when pot-bound and dislikes root disturbance, it should only be re-potted when the dire necessity arises.

Hibiscus rosa-sinensis (Chinese Rose) is a bushy plant, with dark-green, glossy leaves and colourful flowers, that measure up to five inches across. There are whites, pinks, reds, oranges and yellows with some blooms single and others double. There is also a very pretty cultivar, *H. rosa-sinensis* 'Cooperi', which has variegated leaves of deep green and light yellow, tinged reddish-pink. Hibiscus thrive in a well-lit room, with full sun when blooming. In the winter, they should be kept fairly dry in a place where the temperature does not fall below 50°F (10°C). During the growing season, they should be well watered and fed occasionally with liquid manure. Occasional spraying should also be carried out to keep the

air moist. In early spring, hibiscus are pruned to induce good bud formation.

Impatiens petersiana (Busy Lizzie) produces its flowers, which are more usually pink, nearly the whole year round. It grows quickly. It must have a sunny position when in flower, otherwise it needs a well-lit position out of the sun, and to be kept warm in the winter, when it should be maintained just moist enough to prevent the leaves wilting. In summer, it should be given ample water and be fed regularly. It pays also to spray it overhead, but as the plant is subject to attacks of mildew, this practice should be discontinued in the winter. To keep it bushy, it can be periodically pinched back. In addition to several dwarf forms, which include 'Baby Grange' and 'Baby Scarlet', there are some very attractive taller varieties, including 'Red Herald', which has large scarlet flowers marked with white. It can be very easily propagated from cuttings.

Nerium oleander (Oleander, Rose Bay). This shrub requires plenty of space. It is a very beautiful, willow-leaved plant, with clusters of fragrant, tubular flowers, measuring no less than three inches across, but every part of it is poisonous. It is

deadly if eaten! The more usual colour is pink, but there are white, yellow and red varieties, and one with variegated leaves. Cuttings root very easily.

It needs a sunny position, with plenty of watering with tepid water, spraying and occasional feeding in the summer. Its wood can be ripened by standing outside as much as possible in the summer. Its winter temperature should not be allowed to fall below 50°F (10°C).

Saintpaulia ionantha (African violet). There is little doubt that the African violet is one of the most spectacular and popular of all house plants. It is a dainty, low-growing plant that forms clumps of velvety, rounded, hair-covered leaves, that are distinctly veined. Their colour is dark green and, with some of the many varieties, their undersides are purple. Its bright flowers, with their brilliant boss of yellow stamens, resemble violets. According to the variety, the colours range from pure white through all shades of pink and mauve to the deepest purple and violet. Saintpaulia stays in flower for several months. African violets are not easy plants to grow, because their demands are exacting, but they can be met by most plant lovers, who have centrally-heated rooms and a

Impatiens Petersiana (below left)

Vriesia Splendens (below right)

Begonia Manicata (bottom left)

Billbergia Windii (bottom right)

Clivia Miniata (right)

Sparmanniana Africana (far right)

certain amount of patience. Their first requirement is a temperature that nevers falls below 60°F (15°C) and is not subject to violent fluctuations. In addition they must have a moist atmosphere, which can be adequately provided by surrounding their pots with moist peat or standing them on a pebble tray (see page 132–3). They must have plenty of water, seemingly all the time because they do not appear to have a resting period. Watering should, however, be done from below or with a very narrow-spouted watering can, because they resent having water on their foliage, stalks and their crowns, which will rot if wet. Small plastic pots are best for them, because in clay pots any leaves coming in touch with their rims when they are damp tend to rot. They should not be exposed to draughts or gas fumes. They also appreciate regular doses of liquid feed.

They demand good light which is not direct sunshine. It has been demonstrated that they require fourteen hours of light every day to be at their best. Fortunately, they are quite happy with artificial light, especially fluorescent, so their requirements can be met even on the darkest day by artificially supplementing the limited daylight.

Although they are difficult to grow, they can be easily propagated by planting up root divisions in spring.

African violets can produce an almost sensational effect when they are planted in bottle gardens and terrariums. They are also delightful as the low-growing components of arrangements.

Sparmannia africana (Indoor Lime Tree) is a delightful evergreen pot plant, which is hardy. It produces a profusion of attractive, sweet-scented, white flowers from January to May. It likes plenty of water and occasional doses of liquid feed during the summer, with spraying during hot weather. It should be put in a well-lit spot, out of the draught, and it does enjoy spells in the summer sun. It grows well in an ordinary room, provided the air is not too dry, and it withstands smoke and gas fumes. It should be kept in shape by pruning after flowering.

Spathiphyllum wallisii (Peace Lily) grows into a clump of slim, pointed leaves on fairly long stems. Its flowers are typical of the spathes of an arum lily, but smaller, and in colour are first light green, then white and finally green. They are very elegant and last about a month. It is easy to grow in a warm, shady position with good humidity. It delights in central heating and does not object to deep shade, but loathes bright sunlight which turns its foliage yellow. *S. wallisii* 'Mona Loa' is a larger version.

Vriesia splendens is a hardy bromeliad. It has twelve- to sixteen-inch long, upright green leaves, slightly curved back at the tip, with blackish cross bands on either side. It produces on a tall stem, a spear-shaped inflorescence, which is bright scarlet, with tubular, yellow flowers growing at the base of the bracts. The flowers soon die, but the bracts keep their brilliant colour for a long time. It requires the same treatment as *Aechmea*.

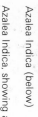

Azalea Indica (below)

Azalea Indica, showing a
particularly beautiful shape
(right)

Azalea Indica with a profusion of
flowers (bottom left)

Cineraria Senecis Cruentus
(bottom right)

Flowering Pot Plants

Flowering pot plants, often called 'florist' or 'gift' plants, play an important role in modern living. During the cold, dark, winter months they provide a very gratifying splash of colour at a time when there are no garden flowers to cut and those available in the florists' are too expensive for many people to buy. There are, in addition, plants that bloom in the spring and summer. It is therefore possible to maintain a form of colour accent in the décor of a room throughout all the seasons.

As has already been explained, the essential difference between house and pot plants is that the leaves of the latter fall and thus, after the flowers fade, they have no decorative value. Many of them are discarded at this point but many with care and attention can be preserved to be attractive once again the following year. Although this is much more difficult for flat-dwellers and those who have no gardens, it can be achieved if storage space is available, particularly if boxes of moderately moist peat, into which the pots can be plunged can be provided and stored in a light, but not sunny place.

The most crucial period in the life of a flowering pot plant is during the days after it has been bought. If the supplier has not kept it under house conditions or in a greenhouse, it is a mistake to bring the plant immediately into a warm room. For about a week, it should be kept in a cool, light place, where the temperature is about 50°F (10°C), with very little watering, although it might be beneficial to spray it with tepid water. If it begins to wilt after this, when put into a warm room, it should be given a few more days under these conditions.

Achimenes (Cupid's Bower) is a tuberous, summer-flowering plant. Its funnel-shaped flowers, which may be white, red or violet, grow from the axils of the leaves. Its slender stalks require staking. It must be kept in a warm, light room, but not in direct sunshine, and watered with moderation, keeping water off its flowers and foliage. It likes, however, a moist atmosphere and does best if its pot is plunged in a second container filled with moist peat. Once it has flowered, it should be allowed to dry out, its stems cut down and, if desired, the tubers removed for re-potting in spring. The latter need a temperature of 65°F (18°C) to start them into growth.

Astilbe (Spiraea). These plants bear large plumes of white, pink or red flowers, which rise above their light-green foliage. They are not difficult to grow if they are placed in a room where there is plenty of sun and are watered freely when coming into flower. After flowering, the more hardy astilbe, such as *Astilbe rosea*, and the varieties 'Peach Blossom' and 'Queen Alexandra' can be transferred to the garden and dug up and re-potted in early spring. The more tender *A. japonica* should be plunged into the soil and brought indoors again before the frost comes.

Azalea indica. The many varieties of Indian azaleas are the most valuable of all flowering house plants, because they are laden with red, pink or white blooms during the winter months. Many people find them difficult to grow in the house, but success can be attained if they are kept in a well-lit, airy spot, out of direct sunlight. They need to be kept fairly warm and out of draughts. It is advantageous to surround the pot with damp peat (see page 132–3). They require to be kept continuously moist and are best watered by allowing the pot to stand up to the rim in water. It is also beneficial to feed them regularly during the blooming season. If the dead flowers are removed without any delay, the flowering season is lengthened.

A. indica can be preserved by plunging the pot into the soil out of doors in May, after the danger of frost has passed. Here it can remain until autumn. When it is necessary to re-pot, a good medium is lime-free, sterilized soil containing a proportion of pine-needle peat.

Begonias. Most of the hybrid begonias with their large, colourful flowers provide a splendid summer and autumn display. Christmas Begonias, Gloire de Lorraine varieties (see page 68), are winter flowering. Begonias are fairly easy to grow if they are kept in a room with good light, at a temperature of not lower than 55°F (13°C) and are watered freely when in flower. They object to gas fumes.

Calceolaria (Slipper Flower). Grown in pots, calceolaria usually flower in spring and summer and, after fading, are discarded. They are dwarf plants with large clusters of red, orange or yellow flowers, with distinctive markings and large, oval-shaped, pointed, rich green leaves. They need cool, airy, well-lit conditions, out of direct sunlight. A shady window-sill is ideal. They should be watered freely and fed with liquid manure occasionally when in flower.

Camellia. These evergreen, hardy shrubs with their handsome, glossy, dark-green leaves and delightful, wax-like flowers will grow for many years in quite small pots. They like much the same conditions as Indian azaleas. They benefit quite considerably from being stood out of doors in a shady spot from early summer onwards. They have, of c urse, all the qualities of a flowering house plant, but they are included in this section because in one respect they can be regarded as 'expendable'. It is an excellent plan to buy a well-budded plant just after Christmas and have the pleasure of it in the house for about two months. After this it is kept in a cool place and ultimately planted out, after it has been hardened off, when there is no more fear of frost.

Chrysanthemums. Because of modern lighting techniques, the potted chrysanthemums are nowadays available in flower throughout the year. Many of them are usually garden varieties, that have been treated with dwarfing compounds to make them short-growing, bushy and compact. They all need to be stood in cool, well-lit, but sunless places, where there is a good air circulation. They should be regularly watered so that the soil does not dry out. It should be remembered that if any chrysanthemums that have been artificially dwarfed are subsequently planted out in the garden, they grow to a normal height.

Cineraria (Senecio cruentus) is a popular shrub with daisy-like flowers of almost every colour except yellow, which appear in winter and spring. It is difficult to surpass them for their decorative beauty. It is not a difficult plant if it is put in a cool, draught-free room with a good light away from direct sun. It should be well watered and given an occasional feed when it is flowering. It is thrown out after flowering.

Coleus (Flame Nettle). This is a plant that is usually expendable. It has the most beautiful multi-coloured leaves. It is difficult to grow because it needs to be kept in well-lit, draught-free rooms, at a temperature never below 55°F (13°C) in a continuously humid atmosphere.

Cyclamen persicum (Persian Violet). This winter-flowering plant, with its heart-shaped, grey, green, silver or mottled leaves and profusion of white, pink, salmon-pink, crimson or cerise flowers, ranks with azaleas for beauty among flowering

Poinsettia

Calceolaria Multiflora Nana (left)

Calceolaria Darwinii (below left)

Cyclamen Persicum (below)

Cyclamen Silver Leaf (below right)

pot plants. It prolongs the display of winter colour for some weeks after the latter have faded.

Unfortunately, not everybody finds it easy to grow, because it dislikes a dry atmosphere which does not rise above 50°F (10°C) in temperature. It should be regularly watered, but always by standing the pot in water so that the crown is not wetted, otherwise it will rot. It likes to be fed regularly during flowering; and to be dead-headed continuously while in flower.

It is possible to make *C. persicum* available the following winter. After flowering, the watering should be lessened and feeding stopped. In the spring the pot should be put out into the garden in a shady position and brought into the house in late summer. If it has to be re-potted, the corm should stand out slightly above the surface. The soil used should be lime-free compost.

Erica (Cape Heath). There are several very colourful cape heaths that appear as pot plants in the winter, representative of several hundred that flourish in S. Africa. Unfortunately, they are not hardy enough to withstand the winter out of doors and are difficult to grow indoors because they drop

their leaves when the conditions do not suit them. They must have good light, a cool situation away from draughts, and plenty of water, preferably rain or soft water, so that the soil never dries out. The atmosphere surrounding the plant must be kept moist (see page 132–3).

Gloxinia. Being essentially a greenhouse plant, gloxinia growing in a house needs to be put in a warm spot, out of the full sun, with a moist atmosphere and soil that is always kept moist. Watering should always be done from the bottom so that the flowers and foliage are not damaged. It likes regular feeding during flowering. It has large trumpet-shaped flowers, which, according to the variety, are rich crimson, deep red, white, violet and various combinations of such colours, and very beautiful, long, broad, pointed, downy, mid-green leaves.

Hydrangea. This plant, which has large heads of white, pink or blue flowers and pleasing green leaves, is a very attractive adjunct to the interior decoration. To be at its best, it likes to be in a room which is well lit, but away from direct sunshine. There should be no draught, and it should be kept fairly warm. During its flowering period, it should be given abun-

A Gloxinia hybrid (left)

Hydrangea Hortensis (below left)

Erica Snowfall (below right)

Calceolaria Herbeo hybrid (left)

Cineraria Maxima Multiflora
Hansa (below left)

Chrysanthemum Festival (below
right)

Cineraria Erfurt (bottom left)

A large-flowered variety of
Cineraria (bottom right)

dant water and an occasional feed. When it has ceased to flower, it is usually discarded by being planted in the garden, but when this is done it often does not bloom for about two seasons.

Pelargoniums. The most popular and easiest to grow of these is *Pelargonium zonale* (Geranium), of which there are many varieties of the different colours and leaf patterns with which most people are familiar. Their needs are pure air and a place in a warm, sunlit, dry, airy room. A window-sill facing south is ideal. Usually they are discarded after flowering.

Poinsettia (*Euphorbia pulcherrima*). This is a difficult plant to grow in most rooms and one that is never very successfully kept from one year to the other. This is unfortunate because it is such a beautiful creation. Its great feature is the large star-shaped groups of scarlet bracts that surround its insignificant small yellow flowers, and that contrast so vividly with its dark-green, pointed leaves. It is usually at its best at Christmas-time. It requires a moist, fairly warm atmosphere, to be free from draughts and gas fumes, and to stand in a good light. It benefits appreciably from its pot being surrounded with damp peat and occasional spraying of its leaves. An improved form is *Poinsettia mikkelrochford.*

Primula is a very popular flowering pot plant. There are a number of attractive species, all of which have a lengthy flowering season. There is quite a range of colours among the more common ones. *Primula kewensis* has small, scented, deep-yellow flowers; those of *P. malacoides* are also small and light purple in colour; *P. obconica* has large rose, blue, red, white or salmon-pink blooms; and those of *P. sinensis* are large and either pink, lilac or white. It should be noted that some people are allergic to *P. obconica*, which can give rise to skin trouble.

To be successful, primulas should be placed in a well-lit, draught-free room, away from heat and direct sun. They need plenty of water during flowering. Dead-heading ensures a long succession of brilliantly coloured blooms. They also react well to regular feeding.

Normally primulas are discarded after flowering, but *P. obconica* and *P. sinensis* can be kept from one season to another if they are allowed to stand in a cool, bright room.

Solanum capsicastrum (Winter Cherry). This gay, delightfully coloured shrub, with its pointed green leaves, and intriguing shiny orange or red berries, brings great cheer to any room, particularly in the winter, when it is in great demand. If it is kept in a cool atmosphere, free from draughts and gas fumes, the berries will stay on the bush for months. Great care must be given to watering, because the leaves will fall if the soil dries out completely or becomes waterlogged. Its leaves should be regularly sprayed. Doses of liquid manure, at intervals during the time the shrub is berried, are advantageous.

Roses. (See page 87.)

Solanum Capsicastrum (below)

Erica Gracilis (bottom)

Gloxinia (right)

Overleaf: Solanum Pseudocapsicum Variegata

Copper Delight

Growing Roses Indoors

It is usually during the winter that many people buy or receive as presents flowering house plants such as cyclamen and azaleas, which give a gorgeous display of colour for perhaps two months, looked after carefully. When these plants fade, their owners wonder what they should buy to take their place. It is always possible to acquire another azalea, but even that will only last a few more weeks. Perhaps roses are the best plants to follow on. It is not always appreciated how easily these popular plants will grow in containers both indoors and out of doors. In some ways they are more beautiful than ever if grown in a greenhouse or in the house, particularly when compared with roses in the open garden, because their blooms are completely unblemished by the ravages of pests and diseases and the effects of bad weather. Greenfly can generally be kept at bay by spraying with clean water, caterpillars can be easily picked off by hand, black spot seldom seems to attack roses grown under cover, and rust never. The only possibility is that the roses might be affected by mildew, which can be dealt with by spraying with a commercial fungicide.

If the roses are to bloom in spring, a start must be made in early autumn. There are quite a number of both floribunda and hybrid tea roses that respond quite well to this treatment. In fact, it might be said that almost every variety is satisfactory. So there is no real problem of selection. There are two approaches. The first is to buy a bare root plant from a nursery and, after trimming away any unruly roots, to plant it in an eight-inch pot in John Innes Compost No.4, to which has been added a small quantity of John Innes Base Fertilizer, both of which are fairly easily obtained from garden supply shops or through mail ordering. If a clay pot is used, a one-inch layer of crocks should be placed at the bottom to assist drainage, which is not necessary in the case of plastic pots. The soil should be tamped down and filled to about an inch from the rim to allow space for watering. The alternative is to go to a garden centre and select a container-grown rose, which has a root ball of such a size that it will fit comfortably into an eight-inch pot. Any space around the outside should be filled with John Innes compost so that the soil is fairly tight. After planting, it should be well watered. It is then allowed to stand outside for about a month, when it should

be brought indoors.

Provided the soil is moist, little more has to be done until mid-winter. If it is not, it should be moderately watered. At this time the rose should be pruned. This is done by first removing all the dead, weak and diseased shoots and any that are growing towards the centre. After this the remaining shoots are hard pruned, that is, cut back to an outgrowing bud, which is the second or third from its base. Incidentally, at the same time every year, potted roses should be similarly treated.

During the next few months, temperature control is important. When producing roses in pots, it is a good idea to be guided as far as possible by the rules laid down by the growers who raise them in greenhouses, which is to keep them at a temperature which is equivalent to that outdoors two months ahead in time. This might be regarded as 50°F (10°C) by day and 46°F (8°C) by night towards the end of winter; 60°F (15°C) and 50°F (10°C) respectively in early spring, and 65°F (18°C) and 55°F (13°C) respectively later in spring. While it might not be possible to adhere strictly to these levels in a house, where there are no strict controls as there are in a greenhouse, to get the best results an endeavour should be made to do so. What it really amounts to is that it is necessary to move the rose from a cooler to a warmer spot as the weeks pass by. Remember that no roses want to be molly-coddled but it is important to see that they are kept in a well-lit place, where there are no draughts, although ventilation from a slightly open window on days when it is not extremely cold, is welcomed by them.

Late in spring, the most perfect blooms will appear. Apart from their decorative value, flower arrangers appreciate them very much, because they can impart an unusual, out of season look to their arrangements.

When they have ceased blooming, all the dead flowers should be removed and the pots put outside in semi-shade in early summer. Here they can remain until autumn, with little attention other than watering if the soil becomes very dry, and having any flower buds removed as they form. Each pot should then be dressed by replacing the top inch of soil with a commercial potting compost plus a little base fertilizer. At the beginning of winter, the pots are brought indoors

Edel (left)

Lilac Charm (right)

again to prepare themselves for another gorgeous display in the following spring.

Regarding varieties, the following hybrid tea roses are proved because they are grown for the florist trade: 'blue' 'Sterling Silver', apricot-yellow 'Dr Verhage', red and gold 'Katherine Pechtold', red 'Montezuma' and vermilion 'Baccara'. Already beloved of British flower arrangers there is also pinky peach, 'Sweet Promise', ('Sonia', as it is called on the Continent). Among the floribunda roses, that are very attractive when grown indoors, are 'Lilac Charm', yellow 'Allgold', 'Copper Delight', carmine-pink 'Paddy McGredy' and crimson 'Red Wonder', but perhaps the most superb of all are the 'Garnette' roses, which can be obtained in a range of the loveliest colours, and are characterized by the long-lasting powers of their blooms, both when on the bush and in water.

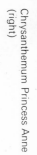

Chrysanthemum Princess Anne (right)

Gloxinia (below left)

Cyclamen Persicum (below right)

Poinsettia (bottom left)

Azalea Indica (bottom right)

Hydrangea Hortensis (far right)

Growing Bulbs Indoors

Nothing brings greater joy than to have spring flowers flourishing in the house during the winter. Some people are eminently successful in growing bulbs indoors, while others fail miserably. There is, however, little for the latter to fear if a few simple rules are faithfully adhered to.

Most commonly grown bulbs are expendable and only serve to give a display once, after which they have to be planted in the garden. There are a few bulb plants that are permanent house plants and more details of these may be found on page 97.

When buying bulbs it is important to buy first-class quality. It must also be realized that bulbs that will be in bloom on Christmas Day have been specially cultivated and stored under controlled conditions of humidity and temperature, which develop the embryo bud in the bulb.

There are several methods of indoor cultivation. Hyacinths and crocuses, for instance, can be grown in the familiar, specially designed bulb glasses, which have an annular shelf in the upper portion on which the bulb can rest. The lower part is filled with water, containing a few pieces of charcoal, at first to a level that touches the bulb. It is then kept in the dark for about eight weeks, by which time the roots will have formed. From this time onwards, the water level is lowered so that there is an air space above it, which prevents the bulb rotting. The glass is then placed in semi-shade for a few days before being moved to a lighter position.

A type of narcissi, bunch-flowered narcissi, can be grown on pebbles in water. A layer of pebbles is placed in a bowl to a height that is two inches below its rim. On this the bulbs are stood and supported with more stones placed between them and the container nearly filled. Water, preferably rainwater, containing a little charcoal, is put in to a level just below the bottom of the bulbs. This should be done in early autumn. The bowl is placed in a cool place (about 45°F (7°C)), either dark or light for about six months. After this, the plants should be given an airy position on a window-sill at a steady temperature of 50°–55°F (10°–13°C). It should not be near a radiator. By mid-winter they should bloom and continue to do so for a long time afterwards.

Lastly, of course, bulbs are commonly planted in indoor bowls and other containers. The growing medium is usually specially prepared bulb fibre, which is essential in pots that have no drain holes.

When planting bulbs, the depth at which they should be placed often worries people. A good guide is for hyacinths, daffodils and narcissi to have their noses just visible, tulips to be *just* covered and small bulbs to have their tips ¼ to ½ inch below the surface.

Planting Bulbs in Containers

Although there may be some small variations, which are mentioned later under the bulb concerned, it is possible to lay down a standard planting procedure that is likely to be successful for most bulbs. The different stages, which are shown in the photographs on page 98 are as follows:

Moist, but not soggy, bulb fibre is placed in the container to such a height that it will support a bulb standing on it at the correct level on completion of planting.

The bulbs are stood on the fibre, a little way from the edge of the bowl, fairly close together, but not touching.

The spaces between the bulbs and that between them and the sides of the container are gently packed with moist fibre. The bowl is then filled to the necessary height and the fibre firmed in.

The bowl is then 'plunged', i.e. placed in a cool dark place for eight to ten weeks, or until the flower buds show colour in the case of crocuses and other small bulbs. This can be done in various ways. The bulbs can be placed in a cool, shady place in the garden and covered with a few inches of moist, but not wet, peat, sand or soil. A rather tidier way is to make a wooden box of suitable size, into which the bowl is placed and covered with sand or other similar material. In both these cases, the bowl of bulbs should be first put in a well-perforated plastic bag or wrapped in newspaper to keep the fibre clean. Those who have little or no garden can place the bulbs in a *cool*, dark cupboard or cellar; a flat-dweller, with a balcony or suitable paved area, can bury them in a box of moist sand as described above. Failing everything else, the container can be kept in a dark corner covered with an upturned cardboard box or a black, polythene tent.

After spending the appropriate period in the dark, the bulbs, which will by this time have one- to two-inch long

Narcissus February Gold (below left)

Narcissus Barrett Browning (right)

Mixed Narcissi (bottom left)

Early Small Tulips (bottom right)

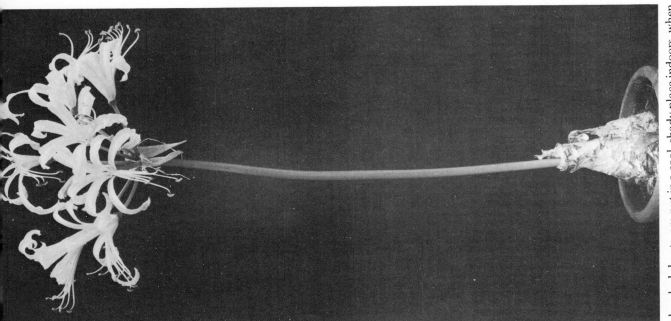
Nerine Bowdenii

blanched shoots, are put in a cool, shady place indoors, when this growth will green up.

Seven days later, they are moved to a warmer, lighter, draught-free position, where they are intended to flower. This should not be near a fire or radiator.

The bulbs should be watered freely, continuing all the time they are in flower. Sometimes staking is necessary. In order to ensure even growth, the bowl should be regularly turned so that all the plants get equal light.

A Selection of Bulbs for Indoor Cultivation

Annual Bulbs. If treated in the above manner, subject to any special modifications indicated, the following bulbs can be successfully grown indoors:

Daffodils, if planted during the summer, will bloom about five months later. They should be plunged for ten to twelve weeks. They they require to be kept in the light at a temperature of 40°–50°F (4.5°–7°C) until the flower buds appear and then at 50°–55°F (10°–13°C).

Crocuses. The *large flowering* types are suitable and very attractive for indoor culture. The spring-flowering crocuses should

be planted during the autumn, and the autumn-flowering in late spring. Both will flower five months after planting. They are kept plunged until the buds just show colour.

Hyacinths. For flowers in mid-winter, the specially prepared bulbs are planted in the summer; for flowering during early spring, they are planted during the autumn. While they are plunged, the temperature should not exceed 45°–50°F (7°–10°C). In about seven weeks, the hyacinths will have thrown up sufficient growth and they are put in a dark cupboard with a temperature of 65°–70°F (18°–21°C) and generously watered. When the flower buds stands well out, the container is transferred for a few days to a place with subdued light, and covered with newspaper to lengthen the flower stem. Any unwanted side shoots and flowering stems are cut off. After this the bulbs can be given more and more light and finally put into their flowering position.

Narcissi. With the specially prepared bulbs, these can be in bloom at Christmas if they are planted in very early autumn and kept in the dark until the beginning of winter. They should then be put into full light and kept at a temperature of 50°–55°F (10°–13°C).

Snowdrops can be in bloom in the house in mid-winter if they are planted in late summer.

Tulips. Suitable varieties, such as Brilliant Star Maximus, Christmas Marvel and Marshal Joffre, can be in bloom in mid-winter if planted in late summer and plunged for three months, when they should be put in a dark place indoors at 65°F (18°C). When their shoots have grown two inches, they should be given light and a steady temperature of 68°F (20°C). If they are required to flower later, they should be planted in early autumn.

Permanent Bulb Plants. The most common among these plants that will last from year to year, are:

Amaryllis (Hippeastrum). The roots and lower part of the bulb are soaked in luke-warm water for several days. Sufficient compost, which is best composed of good loam and leaf-mould, plus a little silver sand, is placed in the container to form a cone, on which the bulb should be stood with its roots spread out. This cone should be of such a height that on completion of planting, the bulb will be half-way out of the soil. The pot is given bottom heat, which encourages development, by placing it on a warm mantelpiece or radiator shelf. When the buds are formed, it should be transferred to a sunny window-sill. For a fortnight afterwards, watering should be sparse and then it should be given tepid water from the top, *never from the bottom.*

After flowering, the plant should be put in a cool place. It should be given water while it grows but once it has finished growing the watering should be gradually diminished to almost nothing during the winter. It should then be put in a cool, frost-free place.

In early spring the pot should be top-dressed with fresh soil and put into a warm place. Watering should be gradually increased. From the time the buds appear until foliage growth stops, it should be regularly fed with liquid manure.

Nerine bowdenii is a very elegant pot plant, that is treated in exactly the same way as an amaryllis.

Vallota speciosa, Vallota purpurea (Scarborough Lily) is a beautiful permanent bulb plant, that has heads of red trumpet-shaped blooms in late summer and elegant foliage that does not die in the winter. Thus, although after flowering, watering should be lessened, it should not cease entirely during the winter. The Scarborough Lily is easy to grow and will remain in the same pot for three or four years. It should be top-dressed with soil in the spring, followed by feeds of liquid manure until flowering time. It likes plenty of sun and water.

a

b

Planting bulbs (right)

(a) Moist bulb fibre is placed in the bowl.

(b) The bulbs are placed in the bowl a little away from the edge.

(c) More moist bulb fibre is worked gently between the bulbs and between the sides of the bowl.

(d) The moist fibre is firmed around the planted bulbs.

(e) The planted bowl is placed in a perforated plastic bag to protect the fibre surface.

(f) The bowl is now ready to be placed in the plunge bed.

c

d

Plunging bulb bowls (above)

(a) A box of suitable depth may hold several bowls.

(b) If the bowls are placed in a box together, their fibre can be protected with a large sheet of plastic.

(c) The plunge bed is then covered with sand.

(d) Finally, the sand is firmed over and the box placed in a cool, dark place.

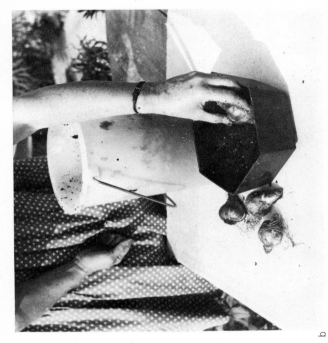

a

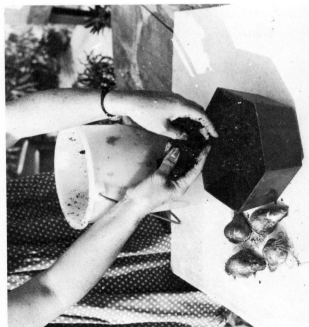

b

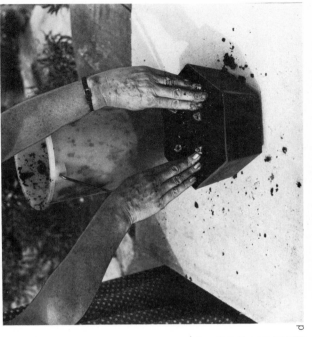

c

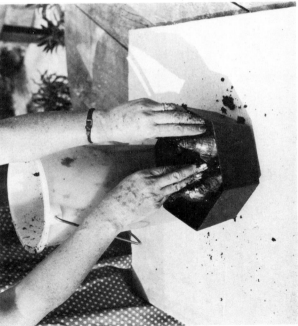

d

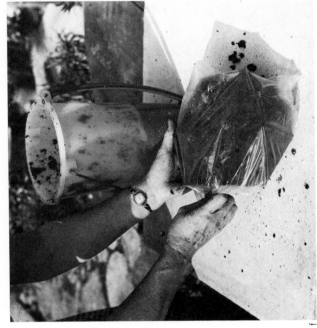

e

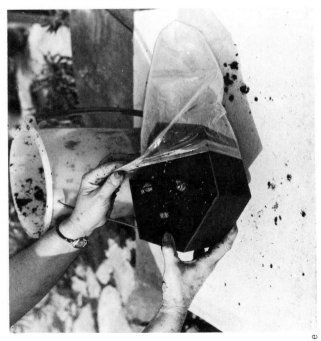

f

Ferns and Palms

oth ferns and palms are foliage house plants, but because they have to some extent different characteristics, it is better to treat them separately. Sixty of more years ago practically no conservatory or front parlour was without its ferns. Even today they are to be found in many houses, and there is every indication that they are returning to popularity. Perhaps it is the cool beauty of their foliage and graceful outlines that creates such a restful atmosphere in contrast to the pressures of modern living, that makes them so acceptable in these times. On the other hand, palms, which one associates with bygone days—the splendour of the pre-war seaside hotel—have an exotic elegance that is appropriate to contemporary, even ultra-modern, décor—undoubtedly the reason why these beautiful, stately plants have come into vogue again in more recent times.

Ferns

There are several thousand species of ferns, but only a very small proportion can be persuaded to grow indoors. Quite a number of them are easy to grow. They are effective in a room as single specimens or as members of a grouping, but they seem to be more appropriate in containers planted only with ferns. Nevertheless, some of the smaller ferns are excellent when planted in bottle gardens and terrariums. They need good light, but mostly abhor bright sunlight. In most cases they like to be kept in a warm place, in which the temperature does not fall below 50°F (10°C). They require a moist atmosphere and, for this reason, they are much happier if their pots are plunged in moist peat or sphagnum moss (see page 132–3). They like to be planted in rich loam, containing at least fifty per cent of peat, which should be kept well watered during their growing period and much drier when they are at rest. They do not like a hot, dry, atmosphere, especially in the presence of gas fumes, because it causes the tips of their fronds to brown.

Adiantum cuneatum (The Maidenhair Fern). There are several attractive varieties, such as 'Dessictum' and 'Grandiceps', and another species that is grown is *A. wrightii*. *A. cuneatum* is not always the easiest of ferns to grow. It is not so particular regarding temperature, but it benefits by being given spells in the warm, moist atmosphere—if it were possible—of a green-

house but, more likely, of a steam bath (see page 132–3). It has a very dainty appearance with each leaf being made up of numerous fan-shaped leaflets, which are carried on thin stems. It is very good in a bottle garden.

Asparagus Fern (*Asparagus plumosus* and *A. sprengeri*). Although neither of these are true ferns, they are regarded as such by most people. Both are climbing plants and have feathery foliage; if lopped they can be kept reasonably low-growing. There is, however, a dwarf variety, *A. plumosus* 'Compactus' which is excellent for small pots. Asparagus fern is treasured by florists and flower arrangers alike because it makes such a beautiful foil to almost any flowers.

Asplendium nidus avis (Bird's Nest Fern). This plant, which is one of the most striking of all indoor ferns, is characterized by its glossy, bright-green, undivided fronds with slightly undulated margins, set in a fashion that has been likened to a shuttlecock. Its leaves grow eventually to about twenty-four inches long and are three to eight inches wide. It does not like bright sun, but it needs more light and warmth than most ferns, and it appreciates a moist atmosphere.

Cyrtomium falcatum (House Holly Fern, Shield Fern). This almost hardy fern is most valuable because it grows well in an ordinary living-room, providing it does not cool to too great an extent at night. It has shining, dark-green, toothed leaves that makes it a fine, decorative plant that contrasts well with the more delicate-looking ferns that are grown indoors.

Nephrolepis exaltata (*N. exaltata bostoniensis*, Boston, Curly, Crested Ladder, Sword or Whitman Fern) is one of the most beautiful ferns for growing either in a pot or hanging basket. It has cascading fronds that are much divided and grow up to three feet long. It likes a good deal of water through the year and pays for feeding during the summer. It lends an elegant accent to any room and will fill an empty corner with a permanent fountain of rich green foliage.

Pellaea rotundifola is a small fern that is very effective in a bottle garden, hanging basket and pot. It forms rounded clumps and has eight-to ten-inch long fronds, that give off up to twenty stalks, each of which carry small, dark-green, round secondary leaves.

Phyllitis scolopendrium, *Scolopendrium vulgare* (Hart's Tongue Fern). This is a hardy fern that grows wild. There are quite

01

a few varieties grown as house plants. They all have strap-shaped fronds, six to eighteen inches long, with wavy edges. Some are crested, and some have variegations or markings in varying shades of green. An additional asset to their great charm is their ability to stand even freezing rooms. They must, however, be kept very moist and out of direct sunshine.

Platycerium bifurcatum, P. alcicorne (Stag's Horn Fern) is an Australian epiphytic, evergreen fern, which means that in its natural habitat it grows on the bark of trees without being planted in soil. Because of this it can be used for decoration in unusual ways. Provided it is kept moist, it will grow very satisfactorily on a pad of moss tied to cork bark, which can be fixed, say, to a wall or anywhere else where the fern will be decorative. It seems to require little feeding.

This spectacular fern has two kinds of leaves, the antler-like, light-green ones that stand out proudly like the horns of a stag, and the large, round, first pale-green and downy, and later brown and papery ones, that attach the plant to its support. It can stand quite low temperatures, but it must be kept out of hot sunshine.

Pteris cretica (Ribbon Fern, Brake Fern) is a fairly quick-

growing fern and easy to grow in almost any room. Its fronds are divided into segments, as if they have been cut from ribbons of stiff green material. It is a handsome fern for a pot. It does not object to bright light and will prosper on a sunny window-sill. In a very hot position, however, it likes a very moist atmosphere. It needs very good watering during the summer and only slightly less in the winter. *P. cretica*, together with its close relatives, *P. argyraea* and *P. ensiformis* 'Victoriae', which has variegated foliage, are very suitable subjects for bottle gardens.

Selaginella (Creeping Moss). These plants are not strictly ferns, but are closely related to them. There are three species which are usually sold by florists. The first is *Selaginella apus*, which has bright-green, prettily shaped leaves; the second is *S. martensii*, with mossy, bright-green foliage; and *S. krauss-siana*, which has bright-green, fern-like foliage. With its twelve-inch trailing stems, the latter is an excellent choice for a hanging basket. Perhaps even more lovely is its variety 'Aurea' which has tiny golden leaves.

Selaginellas require damp, shady conditions and moderate warmth, with a winter temperature of about 55°F (13°C).

Palms

Palms, when young, make good house plants with their plumes of beautiful green leaves. Most of them must be sited in a good light room, but they can manage without sun. They are better if they are kept slightly pot-bound. Top dressing in spring, by replacing half an inch of the existing top layer of soil with fresh leaf-mould, is much appreciated by them. They should be well watered in the summer and sparingly in the winter. They like to be kept out of draughts with a winter temperature never falling below 50°F (10°C).

The more popular palms that are grown indoors are:

Chamaerops humilis (The Fan Palm) is almost hardy and easy to grow. It does best, therefore, in cool or only moderately warm rooms. It is an evergreen shrub, growing up to eight feet tall and producing a clump of stiff, fan-shaped leaves on long stems.

Chamaedorea erumpens (The Bamboo Palm) is a slender, but tall-growing palm and is very suitable for a narrow alcove. It tolerates dry air, provided its roots are kept moist.

Cocos weddelliana, Syagrus weddelliana (The Coconut Palm) grows slowly. It has very stiff, narrow leaves. It needs a minimum winter temperature of 70°F (21°C). Also liking shade, high humidity and moist soil, it thrives in a bottle garden.

Cycas revoluta (The Sago Palm) has ornamental, feather-shaped, dark-green leaves.

Howea belmoreana, Kentia belmoreana (The Curly Palm). This species and *H. forsteriana* (Kentia Palm) are generally considered the best palms for growing in pots and for use in living-rooms. The temperature during the winter should not fall below 45°F (7°C) for both of them. They eventually become large and tall and need a large pot. They both have graceful, feathery leaves.

Neanthe bella, Neanthe elegans (The Parlour Palm) is an excellent small palm for both dish and bottle gardens.

Phoenix dactylifera (The Date Palm) grows up to sixty feet high in its natural surroundings, but makes a very lovely house plant when planted in a pot. Its leaves are a bright green. It can be raised from date stones (see page 137).

P. roebelinii is the species that is more often seen in florists. It is a very elegant and striking house plant. The leaves, which are feathery and shiny and dark green in colour, have leaflets that are sometimes sickle-shaped. The richness of its green can be retained by placing a lump of sulphate of iron on the surface of the soil and allowing it to dissolve during the course of watering. It needs to be kept warmer than *P. dactylifera.* Its winter temperature should not fall below 60°F (15°C).

Rhapis excelsa, R. flabelliformis (The Lady Palm) has fan-shaped, deep-green leaves, which can be kept dark with sulphate of iron (see above). It can stand low temperatures and prefers shade.

106

Cacti and Succulents

I t will be noted that the terms 'cacti' and 'succulents' are both used in the title of this chapter. This is unavoidable when dealing with this subject, because it has become the practice to regard these as two groups of plants, but technically it is wrong to speak of 'cacti' and 'succulents' because cacti themselves are succulents. Succulents are by definition plants that have originated in habitats where long periods of drought are experienced, calling for them to survive without water. This they do by becoming adapted so that they can reduce the loss of water by evaporation from their tissues and store water. This is done by developing thick, fleshy tissues within their stems and/or leaves, that are enclosed by a thick skin or bark. Another device that these plants have developed in order to give them the power to conserve their water supplies is to adopt shapes that have the maximum volume with the minimum surface area, so that evaporation from the latter is minimized. In consequence, succulents tend to be rounded in shape, because, as the mathematicians among the readers will appreciate, a sphere meets this condition to the fullest extent, i.e. it has the largest volume in relation to its surface area of all shapes.

Many succulents have no leaves, but their normal functions, such as transpiration and converting water and carbon dioxide, with the aid of sunlight and chlorophyll, are carried out by the green fleshy tissues of the stems. It is important to appreciate fully that certain plants have evolved these succulent properties over the ages because of the living conditions in which they have found themselves. In consequence, there is no specific family of succulents. Plants with succulent qualities are found to be members of at least twenty widely varied plant families. Some have only a few succulents, while the others, such as the cactus family, are entirely composed of them. On the other hand, others such as aloes and haworthia, which belong to the lily family, the kleinias, which are compositae, and agave, a member of the narcissus family, are distributed through a range of botanical families.

While dealing with definitions it should be pointed out there are two types of cacti popular for interior decoration. The first is known as Desert Cacti and, as their name suggests, they are the ones found living in the hot, arid conditions of the desert. The second type is known as *Epiphytes*. In their natural

habitat they grow on trees and rocks. They are not parasites, but derive nutriment from decaying vegetable matter. Some of the latter species have been highly developed and there are now available some very lovely flowering hybrids, a number of which are scented.

Cultivation

Generally speaking, succulents enjoy an open soil that drains very quickly. The desert or terrestrial type like a growing medium, comprised of equal parts of sifted heavy loam, coarse sand and a mixture of four parts finely broken brick and one part old mortar rubble. Epiphytic cacti prefer their soil to include very generous proportions of sifted peat and well-rotted cow manure added to the above medium. Of them, the epiphyllum cacti in particular dislike excess lime, so it is as well to omit the mortar rubble in their case.

Desert cacti like a very sunny position, whereas the epiphytes, because they grow naturally in woodlands, need less sun, but in order to ensure that they bloom well they should be in the sun for part of the day. For the same reason, they like to be watered *freely*, particularly in the spring when the buds are forming, but after flowering is over they should not be watered for about a month in order to give them a rest. When this period has passed watering should be resumed. While they should not be allowed to dry out, they do not need water during the winter, particularly if they are placed in a cool position. Desert cacti in their natural surroundings are subject to heavy rain and the soil dries out before more comes. They are therefore not used to having their roots in soil that remains damp for long periods. To simulate these conditions, desert cacti should be watered regularly during spring and summer, but the compost should be allowed to dry out before watering is repeated. It has been shown that this alteration of wet and dry spells encourages flowering. Like epiphytic cacti, they should be given very little water during the winter.

Although desert cacti enjoy high temperatures in the summer, they can be kept at quite a low temperature in the winter, providing they do not freeze, but in the case of epiphytes, the temperature should not fall below 45°F (7°C).

Cacti are able to withstand to a small extent gas and other obnoxious fumes. They do, however, tend to get dusty, parti-

Astrophytum Myriostigma (below)

An attractive variety of Epiphyllum (right)

cularly when they are knobbly and bristly. They are best cleansed by stroking with a soft brush. Their containers should be turned regularly in order to prevent uneven growth.

Cacti are generally easy to grow and, in the case of many, to multiply. They will resist a considerable amount of neglect. They are therefore ideal for house plants, when spare time is limited. A large number of them are dwarf and have small growth patterns, so that they are invaluable for table decorations in places where thee space is restricted. They also make the most interesting and attractive dish gardens, but because of their soil requirements and growing conditions being different to those of most other indoor plants, they should not be mixed with them.

A Selection of the More Popular Cacti and Other Succulent Plants
Aeonium haworthii is easy to grow and increase by stem cuttings. It carries rosettes of leaves at the top of its stems. It makes an attractive bush. Other species suitable for indoor pot culture are *A. arboreum* and *A. tabuliforme*.
Agave americana 'Variegata'. Although this plant will flower after many years, it is grown for the loveliness of its leaves, which are striped green and yellow. It is easy to grow and is commonly known as the Century Plant or American Aloe.
Aloe variegata (Partridge-breasted Aloe, Falcon Feather, Tiger Aloe) is mainly attractive for its rosettes of triangular-shaped,

grey-green leaves with whitish spots. It grows easily to an eventual height of twelve inches and is robust. *A. arborescens*, *A. brevifolia* and *A. humilia* are other aloes recommended for pot culture.

Astrophytum myriostigma (Bishop's Mitre). This pleasant green-skinned plant with white felted flecks is easy to grow. It normally has five ribs and grows large yellow flowers, usually from the crown.
Cephalocereus senilis. It is commonly called 'Old Man Cactus', because of the long, wavy, silver-grey and whitish hair with which it is covered.
Cereus jamacaru. This desert cacti is an intriguing angular, columnar plant with bluish-coloured stems. It rarely flowers indoors, but being rather taller, it is an attractive accent plant in an arrangement.
Ceropegia woodii (Hearts Entangled). This succulent plant is a trailer, which is mainly grown for its foliage. Its leaves, which are heart-shaped, grow in pairs along its long, reddish-brown stems. The upper surfaces of the leaves are dark green with a heavy grey mottle, making them appear silvery.
Chamaecereus silvestrii (Peanut Cactus). It is a good species for a beginner. It has cylinder-shaped, prostrate stems or branches, pale green in colour with soft spines. In early summer it produces funnel-shaped, orange-vermilion flowers, which grow direct from these branches. It should be kept cold (32°F (0°C) will not harm it) during the winter.

Cotyledon undulata. This succulent plant has the most attractive large leaves, which are narrowed at the base and fan out with a wavy edge. They are covered with white powdery bloom, which gives them a pretty, greyish look. The plant should not be watered from above, otherwise this is washed off. Its flowers are pendant and bell-shaped and cream with red stripes in colour.

Crassula arborescens (Tree Crassula) is a tallish plant, which is a good accent in a dish garden. Its leaves are greyish-green and dotted red.

C. perforata, with its greyish-green leaves strung like beads along its prostrate stems, *C. argentea* and small-growing, tree-shaped *C. lycopodioides,* with its square stems covered with tiny green leaves, are also recommended for pots.

Echeveria glauca (*E. secunda glauca*) has beautiful glaucous rosettes of blue-green, margined red leaves, from which rise on arching stems its bright red and yellow flowers. It makes an excellent centre-piece for an arrangement. Other eche-veria that grow successfully indoors are *E. derenbergii, E. ful-gens* (*E. retusa*) and *E. pulvinata.*

Echinocactus grusonii (Barrel Cactus, Hedgehog Cactus) is a popular, golden-spiked, round-shaped cactus, which seldom flowers indoors, but is nevertheless very decorative.

Echinocereus blanckii. Although upright when young, its dark green, 12–14-inch long and over 1 inch in diameter branches eventually become prostrate. They have groupings of 8 or 9 black or white spines. It is very beautiful with its abundant, 4-inch long, violet flowers. It is hardy and will sometimes grow outdoors, but needs good light. A slower growing species, *E. gelmannii,* is appreciated for its thick covering of yellow to red-brown spines.

Echinopsis eyriesii. This is a very easy-to-grow favourite. When young it is almost spherical in shape with a dark, shiny green skin with spines on its ribs. Its flowers are white and grow at the top of high stems.

Epiphytic Cacti

Aporocactus flagelliformis (Rat's Tail Cactus) has long, glossy, green, later grey-green, narrow stems, from which emerge three-inch long reddish-purple flowers, usually at the beginning of spring.

Epiphyllum ackermannii (Orchid Cactus) and its varieties. This is a highly developed epiphyte. The species has finely scalloped, dark-green leaves (actually they are flattened stems), with very few spines and produces the most gorgeous, very large, deep-crimson flowers. It has a number of very attractive hybrids.

Rhipsalidopsis rosea (Easter Cactus) is like a miniature Christmas Cactus (see below).

Rhipsalis houlletiana has long, thick stems, which can be either supported or allowed to hang over the side of a container. It

Aporocactus Flagelliformis in flower (left)

Chamaecereus Silvestrii (below left)

A cultivar of Epiphyllum (below right)

Epiphyllum Oxypetalum (bottom right)

is rounded at the bottom and flattened at the top. It has serrated edges from which its creamy-white flowers, with a red eye, spring. They are followed by red berries.

Schlumbergera gaertneri, more recently termed *Rhipsalidopsis gaertneri* (Whitsun Cactus). It has the same habit as *Zygocactus truncatus* (see below). Its leaf-like green stems have purplish, notched edges and not many bristles. Its scarlet and violet flowers appear in late spring. Another attractive species is *Schlumbergera bicolor*, which flowers in the winter.

Zygocactus truncatus is the very popular Christmas Cactus, so called because at that time it flowers at its best. It is a pendulous, spreading plant with long segmented stems, from the terminals of which grow vivid cerise-pink flowers.

Euphorbia splendens (Crown of Thorns) is a shrubby plant with brown, branching spikes. It has bright-scarlet bracts surrounding tiny yellow flowers. It is deciduous, but *E. bojeri* is evergreen and flowers most of the year.

Gasteria verrucosa is a favourite succulent plant. It is tufted and has two ranks of thick, fleshy, three-sided, dull-grey leaves, with whitish wart-like protuberances.

Gymnocalycium quehlianum is the shape of a flattened sphere and has ribs, which are composed of knobs, from which brownish spines radiate. Its skin is dull grey-green, becoming brownish in the sun. At its crown it produces funnel-shaped, whitish flowers, that have a carmine centre.

Kalanchoë blossfeldiana is one of a very large species. It has dark-green, red-edged succulent leaves, from which grow panicles of scarlet flowers on slender, foot-tall stems during the winter. It needs plenty of water during the growing season. *K. kewensis* and *K. tomentosa* are also suitable for growing in pots.

Kleinia articulata (Candle Plant) has attractive glaucous-blue, jointed, half inch thick stems, from which grow small, fleshy, green leaves. Some stems hang over the side of the container. The flowers, which are yellowish, have an unpleasant smell and should be removed.

Mammillaria bocasana. This member of the Mammillaria species, which includes some of the most popular cacti, is commonly known as the Pincushion Cactus. It is a small rounded plant, which produces freely blue to green, short sideshoots, which are completely covered with fine white spines. As a result, the whole mass acquires a bluish-grey colour. Through this covering yellowish flowers with a central reddish stripe on the outer petals, appear. Other species of interest to indoor plant enthusiasts are *M. 'Bicolor', M. elegans* 'Aurei-spina' which has yellow spines, *M. kewensis, M. prolifera* and *M. winteriae*. All these mammillaria are easy to grow.

Opuntia microdasys (Prickly Pear, Bunny's Ears). This is probably one of the most intriguing and charming cactus for growing indoors. It is a shrub-like plant composed of flattened oval pads. They are emerald green in colour. They are

Epiphyllum hybrid (right)

Crassula Lycopodioides (below)

Echeveria Retusa Hybrida
(bottom left)

Cephalocereus Senilis (bottom
right)

Echeveria Levcotricha (below)

Conophytum Pearsonii (below right)

Rebutia Haagei (bottom left)

Echinocereus Blanckii (bottom right)

Aloe Variegata (below)

Zygocactus Truncatus (bottom)

covered regularly in squares with areoles (pincushion-like knobs) from which emerge a large number of very small, yellowish-brown, barbed bristles, giving the plant a woolly appearance. It needs to be very sparingly watered in the winter but otherwise it is a tolerant, easy-to-grow plant. *Pachyphytum oviferum*. Being closely related to the echeverias, this species has rather similar flowers. The leaves, however, are much more fleshy and round. Those of *P. oviferum* are covered in a white bloom, which gives them the appearance of sugar-dusted acid-drops. This is a most attractive feature,

Pebble Plants

These plants, which are all members of the South African mesembryanthemum family, grow naturally among stones, which they closely resemble. There are several that are of interest for growing indoors.

Conophytum pearsonii is, next to Lithops (see below), among these types of plants comparatively easy to grow. It forms unusual clumps of rounded stems, which are broadly conical with a flattened crown. These stems are more like small apples in shape than stems. They are smooth and bluish-green in colour. The flowers, which appear during September and October, the beginning of the growing season, are pale violet in colour. During their resting period *in the summer*, a new body forms inside the old stem, absorbing all the substances from it until all that remains is the skin, which dries and protects the new plant from the heat of the sun and excessive water evaporation. The resting plant during this period looks like a stone. Hence it is known as a 'living pebble'. Another attractive species is *C. bilobum*, which has yellow flowers.

Lithops bella. Before it blooms it looks very much the same as a round pebble. It consists of two fleshy, plump leaves, which are about an inch high. It resembles in shape a roundish pebble that has a very noticeable fissure across its flattened top. In the autmn there grows from this crevice a daisy-like white flower, which is about an inch in diameter. The new leaves grow inside the old ones, exactly as described for *C. pearsonii*.

which must be preserved by taking care that they do not get wet when being watered.

Rebutia marsoneri. The body of this cacti is flattened spherical in shape, ultimately attaining a height of about 2½ inches and a diameter of about 3½ inches. Its colour is pale green with its base eventually becoming grey. With its golden-yellow flowers breaking from intensely red buds, this cacti was a great discovery because hitherto known Rebutias had flowers that were varying shades of red. Another very attractive little plant, which is easy to grow is *R. pseudodeminuta*. It is a flattened sphere no more than 2½inches in diameter. It flowers very abundantly with red and golden flowers just over an inch across. Another that can be recommended for pot culture is *R. haagei*.

Sedum adolphii is a low semi-shrub, which has fleshy or semi-woody branches. Its leaves are fleshy, pale green in colour and oval in shape. They are about 1½ inches long and ¾ inch across. Part of the charm of this plant lies in the delightful manner in which these leaves, growing at the end of each branch, form a close cluster. Other species that make good house plants are *S. allantoides*, which has whitish-green, stout keel-shaped leaves, and *S. pachyphyllum*, with similarly shaped leaves which are green, tipped with red.

Opuntia Microdasys Albispina
(left)

Echeveria Graptopetalum
Weinbergii (below right)

Crassula Lactea (bottom left)

Echeveria Retusa Hybrida
(bottom right)

Overleaf: Cactus dish garden

Miniature Trees and Shrubs

Fagus Crenata, a Bonsai tree
about 40 years old

Another very pleasing and decorative way of having plants indoors is to grow miniature trees and shrubs. They are all fascinating and, as will be discussed later, can give people, who are interested in gardening but have no or little garden, a very absorbing hobby.

The dwarf trees and shrubs that are grown indoors fall into two categories. These are firstly the naturally diminutive ones and, secondly, the artificially dwarfed ones or 'Bonsai'.

Natural Miniatures

It is of interest to discuss for a short time the reasons why dwarf varieties of various species are found growing in nature, because they have some practical bearing on the production of bonsai. Mention should first be made, however, of two other sources of naturally raised miniatures. Firstly, some are obtained by selection of any seedlings that show exceptional dwarf characteristics and secondly, by taking cuttings from 'Witches Brooms' which are dense clumps of stunted twigs appearing on the branches of normal trees and caused by the action of certain insects.

The majority of dwarf trees and shrubs have originated in mountainous and very exposed areas, in which there is poor, shallow soil. This has possibly restricted the growth of their roots, since they are contained by large stones, and high winds and general exposure naturally prune their branches and mould them into strange shapes. They have, under these circumstances, adapted themselves in such ways that they are well equipped to resist adversity. At the same time it should be noted that such plants grow in well-drained soil and are exposed to a great deal of very clean, bright light and to rather cooler conditions; these factors are all useful clues to their cultivation when indoors.

Most miniature trees, whether natural or bonsai, grow best in shallow containers, not only because such a condition is much nearer to that of their habitats, but also because they look more artistic when planted in this way. Good drainage must be assured with ample drainage holes in their pots. If it is desired to plant the dwarfs in ornamental containers which have no drain holes, a good layer of ballast or crocks should be put at the bottom. The addition of a few lumps of charcoal is also an advantage as it helps to minimize sourness.

A good soil, although not too rich, is the best in which to plant the natural dwarfs. Bonsai, however, require an even poorer soil if they are to retain their diminutive stature and they grow better in a mixture of two parts commercial potting compost and one part coarse sand. They require regular watering, but no feeding because this encourages unwanted growth.

Regarding the selection of natural miniature trees and shrubs, the most fruitful source is the dwarf conifers. Among them, there are some most fascinating, shapely, colourful species and varieties; in particular those classified as real pygmies prove delightful for indoor decoration. Anybody interested is advised to pay a visit to one of the specialist nurserymen in the country in order to make their own selection. A few good selections are white variegated, columnar *Chamaecyparis lawsoniana* 'Ellwood's White', *C. pisifera* 'Nana', which is a tight, low bun of dark green foliage, *C. pisifera* 'Nana Aureo Variegata', which has a superb golden sheen, *C. pisifera* 'Plumoso Compressa' which is a perfect gem for a pot, *Cryptomeria japonica* 'Bandai-sugi' which has dense moss-like foliage, grey-leaved, columnar *Juniperus communis* 'Compressa', the globose, blue-foliaged *Picea mariana* 'Nana', the dwarf yew, *Taxus baccata* 'Nutans', *Thuja occidentalis* 'Hetz Midget' which is one of the smallest of all conifers and *T. orientalis* 'Minima', which is exceptionally neat, slow-growing and globose in shape.

Regarding shrubs, the purple *Acer palmatum* 'Dissectum purpureum' and its green counterpart *A. palmatum* 'Dissectum viridis' have been found to be elegant small trees, lasting for many years. Miniature roses, of which there are many varieties, have also been successful. Other attractive dwarf plants that can be seen at leading nurseries are: very dwarf *Cotoneaster dammeri*, evergreen *Daphne collina*, with deep bluish-green leaves and soft purple flowers, evergreen *Pernettya tasmanica*, which only grows two inches tall and has red berries, and *Santolina chamaecyparissus* 'Nana', which has the most distinctive, white, frosted foliage.

Artificially Dwarfed Trees and Shrubs or 'Bonsai'

The bonsai art, which has been practised in Japan and China for many centuries, is well established in the United States

Bonsai Maple (below)

Bonsai Pyracantha (right)

and is becoming steadily increasingly popular in Great Britain. For those whose sole interest is for interior decoration, for which they are most valuable assets, it is possible to buy specimens from florists and specialist nurserymen, and to plant them in specially chosen containers, but some of the larger and very old ones can cost several hundreds of pounds. Dwarfing trees and shrubs can, however, be a most absorbing hobby for both young and old, not only because it is a form of horticultural and artistic interest, but because if it is practised faithfully, it involves the study of the habits of various trees. It is indeed a vast subject and can only be briefly touched upon in this book, but because it is of importance, a short description of the process of producing bonsai is given.

Quite a number of both native and exotic trees and shrubs are responsive to this treatment. In fact, after some experience has been gained, it is worth while trying out any particular favourite. As a preliminary, it might be mentioned that generally plants with small leaves and flowers give dwarfs of good proportion and thus have a correct appearance. An exception to this assertion is that flowers growing in racemes, like those of wistaria and laburnum, are always most attractive. Another factor to be taken into account is that large flowers are not reduced in size.

Centrally-heated, modern rooms with plenty of light make it possible to grow half-hardy dwarf plants such as oleanders and olives, indoors in a sunny window. All bonsai must, however, be kept out of draughts and away from the fire. Spraying with water at room temperature once a week and sponging the leaves occasionally to remove the dust is also appreciated. The hardy dwarfs should also be put out of doors in warm rain as often as possible.

The Dwarfing Process

Trees and shrubs, of which a selection is given below, are started from cuttings or seeds or seedlings found in the garden by planting them in a shallow pan in potting or seed compost. The seeds should be soaked in water for twenty-four hours. The larger ones, such as acorns and beech nuts, should be placed about half an inch down, but smaller seeds less deeply. The pan should be well watered before planting and kept continuously moist. When the cuttings are rooted and the seedlings are two inches high, the dwarfing processes, which are spread over two years, or three in the case of very slow-growing plants, are started. The little plants are transplanted to individual containers, using a commercial potting compost. These can be clay or plastic pots with ample drainage holes. If these are used, during the next two years, the young plants are periodically removed and all the roots growing outside the ball are cut back. As an alternative, they may be planted in cream or ice-cream cartons, in which holes

have been punched in the wall and bottom with a knitting needle. As soon as the roots protrude through the holes, they are cut off. Some growers prefer, as a third alternative, to plant out in the skin of half an orange or grapefruit, which is soft enough to allow the roots to pass through, and then be clipped off.

This process of root pruning continues during the plant's second year, during which time steps are also taken to shape the plant. This is done by pinching out the growing tip with the finger and thumb to encourage it to grow bushy. After this, it is shaped by shortening the shoots one after another and removing completely any undesirable ones. In order to minimize shock, root and shoot pruning should not be carried out simultaneously. Shoot pruning should be aimed at giving a natural outline to the dwarf, similar to that which the large tree would take up on maturity. This process, which must be spread over a continuous period, is best done in spring and summer when growth is at its greatest.

Sometimes it is desired, as the Japanese do, to give the miniature the appearance of premature old age or, perhaps, grotesqueness. This is done by mechanical means, such as curling wire round the branches and trunk, so bending the tree to shape, fixing weights to branches to bear them down and twisting the trunk and limbs by tying them to pegs firmly inserted in the soil.

At the beginning of the third year, after root pruning, the bonsai should be transferred to their permanent quarters in poor soil, composed of two parts potting compost and one part coarse sand. During this year the plants should be pinched back from time to time to regulate their appearance.

Among the plants readily dwarfed artificially are the conifers, abies (firs), monkey-puzzle tree, chamaecyparis, cedars, gingkos, hemlock spruce, junipers, larch, pines, spruce and yews; the suitable evergreen and deciduous trees and shrubs include acacia (including mimosa), beech, birch, buddleia, colutea, crab apples, deutzia, dogwoods (cornus), eucalyptus, hawthorns, holly, horse chestnut, ivies, jacaranda, laburnum, lilac, maples, oleander, olive, philadelphus (mock orange), poplar, prunus (viz. flowering almonds, apricots, cherries, peaches and plums), pyrus, pyracantha, snowberry tree, tamarix, walnut, willows, winter sweet and wistaria.

Pinus Parviflora, about 35 years old

Wistaria (below left)
Chamaecyparis Pisifera
Squamosa (below)
Bonsai, Chamaecyparis Ablusa
Hinoki Cypress (bottom)
Overleaf: Bonsai Acer Seigen
(above left)
Miniature Acer Japanese Maple
(below left)
Dish garden (right)

Dish Gardens, Bottle Gardens and Terrariums

§ingle plants are very valuable in a room, provided they are restricted in number so that they give some sort of emphasis; however, if it is desired to have a display, be it large or tiny, it is better done by grouping plants in one container. Although this has already been mentioned on page 21, it must be stated here once again, that plants chosen for any arrangement must all like the same living conditions. If this vital rule is not adhered to, the dish garden will inevitably be a failure. This does not, however, present any difficulty because although there are numbers of incompatible plants, there are still many left to choose from.

The most attractive arrangements of house plants in a container are those composed of plants varying in height and in growth habit and which have contrasts in foliage shapes and colours. A well-proportioned grouping, generally speaking, should always contain one predominantly tall plant with several bushy ones of varying low heights to act as a foil, and one or two trailers, which will gracefully overhang the sides of the dish. There are two approaches to planting out a dish garden. The first, which applies to a grouping of plants that all like much the same soil conditions, is to knock the plants out of their pots and plant them in compost in the normal way. It is important that when this is done particular care is taken to see that there is good drainage.

The alternative method of making a dish garden is to put into the container a layer of moist peat, on which the individual pots are stood. They are then packed round with more damp peat up to the rims of the pots. This method has the advantages that plants liking different types of soil, but *not different environmental conditions*, can be mixed together; it allows different plants to be given varying levels of watering; in enables flowering pot plants and bulbs to be included in a grouping to give colour at varying times of the year; and it enables some plants to be positioned at an angle if the nature of the arrangement demands it. If necessary, the rims of the pots can be hidden with stone, driftwood or moss.

Miniature gardens, which are rather more complicated because they include small garden features, such as paths, pools, well-heads, etc. and therefore call for some designing, are planted out in the same way as for dish gardens.

There are, of course, many combinations of plants that can be very charmingly used for a dish garden. The final choice must be a matter of personal taste, but a few typical groupings are:

Large-size arrangements

1 Chamaedora elegans 'Bella'
Dracaena sanderi
D. sanderi 'Borenquensis'
Hedera helix 'Scutifolia'
Peperomia obtusifolia 'Variegata'
Sansevieria trifasciata 'Hahnii'
Scindapsus aurea
Syngonium podophyllum

2 Aphelandra squarrosa
Dracaena sanderi
Ficus benjamina
Fittonia verschaffeltii
Hedera canariensis 'Variegata'
Peperomia argyreia
P. hederifolia

Medium-size arrangements

1 Asplenium nidus avis
Dracaena deremensis 'Warnecki'
Grevillea robusta
Peperomia caperata
Poinsettia

2 Calathea ornata
Ficus elastica 'Decora'
Hedera helix 'Glacier'
Neoregelia carolinae 'Tricolor'

Small-size arrangements *(suitable for a pedestal vase)*

1 Hedera helix 'Chicago'
Saintpaulia

2 Chlorophytum capense 'Variegatum'
Begonia rex
Peperomia rotundifolia

Bottle gardens demand some skill but to make them is a very absorbing task. More commonly they are constructed in disused acid carboys, but these are not always easily obtained.

A bowl arrangement of
houseplants (below left)

A wide range of plants lends
shape and colour to a bowl
garden (below right)

Crystal Terrarium (far left)

Of course any large bottle with a wide neck is suitable, provided it is made of white glass so that the occupants receive the maximum light. Yet another type of vessel that can be similarly planted out is a glass terrarium. This usually consists of a ten- or twelve-inch diameter bowl fitted with an air-tight lid. Quite a satisfactory terrarium can be improvised, using a disused battery jar or a goldfish bowl. The advantage of planting in such containers is that they allow delicate plants to be grown, which require a very moist atmosphere, warmth and complete freedom from draughts.

It will be appreciated that a wide-mouthed terrarium is much easier to plant out than a carboy. The latter demands quite a lot of dexterity, but with patience and several improvised tools it can be done. The ultimate results obtained are so beautiful that it is worth while making a great effort to create a bottle garden. It is now proposed to discuss how this is done. It will be appreciated that the same principles apply to other types of bottles, terrariums, and goldfish bowls, but manoeuvring in the last two is very much easier.

As a preliminary to making a bottle garden, it is necessary to provide some tools. Most of these can be improvised by the bottle gardener using two-foot long bamboo canes as handles to the various implements. An excellent substitute trowel can be made by cutting off and straightening a little the handle of an old teaspoon. The end is then stuck in the hollow centre of a bamboo cane, with, if necessary, some packing, using a plastic padding adhesive; likewise, a fork-cum-rake can be constructed from an old table fork. Another valuable planting tool is a rammer, which consists of a spent cotton reel through the centre hole of which is rammed a bamboo cane

smeared with adhesive so that a secure joint is obtained. Tools required for the maintenance of a bottle garden consist of a long-handled pruning knife, which can be constructed by securely mounting a razor blade in the split end of a two-foot long bamboo cane and fixing it with sticky tape. To remove the cuttings and dead leaves a pair of long-handled tongs are required. These might be improvised by shortening the handles of a pair of light kitchen tongs and giving them long bamboo ones. If this is not possible, with practice such debris can be taken away from the bottle with bamboo canes, used in the manner of chopsticks.

The first thing to do when creating a bottle garden is to wash the carboy out thoroughly, since it has usually been previously used to carry strong acid. Copious quantities of detergent and water should be used for this purpose. As it has no means of free drainage, the bottom of the container should be lined with a layer of stones or other crocks.

On top of this must be placed a quantity of moist commercial potting compost. In order to increase the display this may be made sloping, using the fork, from back to front and given some undulations. The compost is then lightly consolidated using the rammer (see illustrations overleaf). The selected plants should next be arranged in their small pots in a bowl of compost with a surface approximately the same in area as that of the soil in the bottle garden. By doing this, a satisfactory grouping can be obtained beforehand because manipulation in a narrow-necked carboy is difficult.

When this has been done, a hole is made with the trowel in the compost in the bottle and the first plant is dropped into this hole and manoeuvred into position using the improvised

tongs or 'chopsticks'. The roots are then covered and the soil firmed round them with the rammer. It is better to commence planting on the outside and work towards the centre. Care should be taken to see that the plants are not squashed against the sides of the bottle, but a few leaves might be allowed just to touch them. Interest can be increased by covering some of the soil with stones or pieces of mossy bark.

All that remains is to water the plant and wash the inside of the glass. This is most effectively done by means of a small cylindrical garden spray, preferably with the nozzle set at an angle, which can be inserted inside the carboy. The soil should be watered and any adhering to the leaves be washed off. Also any adhering to the glass should be removed by means of a sponge attached to a piece of wire.

After the top of the bottle is closed, at first it will steam up, but this will soon clear away. It will not need watering again for at least two months. It should, however, be watched, particularly in the early stages to see that it does not dry out. After a good moisture balance has been established, the bottle garden will only need water occasionally. Depending upon the surroundings, the intervals could be as long as a year.

A selection of plants suitable for Bottle gardens and Terrariums

It is important not to choose strong-growing plants for this purpose. Those given in the following list are suitable:

Acorus gramineus 'Variegatus'
Adiantum cuneatum
Begonia rex
Chlorophytum capense 'Variegatum'
Cocos weddelliana
Codiaeum pictum 'Variegatus'.
C. pictum 'Apple Leaf'
Cryptanthus
Ctenanthes oppenheimiana 'Tricolor'
Cyrtomium falcatum
Dracaena godseffiana
D. sanderi
Ficus pumila
Fittonia verschaffeltii

Helxine soleirolii
Hoya carnosa 'Variegatus'
Ivies
Maranta leuconeura 'Kerchoveana'
Nephrolepis exaltata
Peperomia magnoliaefolia
Pilea cadiera 'Minima'
P. involucrata
Saintpaulias
Sansevieria trifasciata 'Laurentii'
Saxifraga sarmentosa
Selaginellas
Tradescantias

a

c

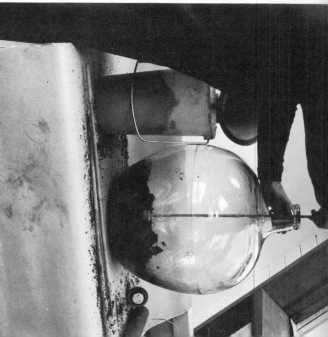

b

d

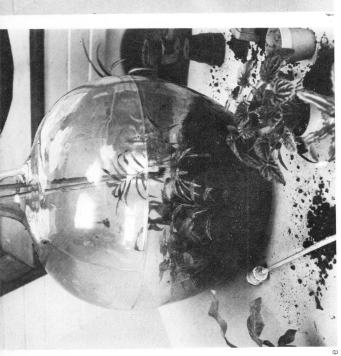

a) The cleaned-out carboy is filled with stones, then with a layer of compost.

b) The compost is consolidated with a rammer.

c) A hole is made for the first plant, using the improvised carboy tools.

d) Planting out the carboy.

e) Manoeuvring plants into position using the tongs.

f) Setting the last plant in place.

g) A final clean-up, using a sponge on wire, removes the last traces of soil from the inside of the glass.

Cultivation of Indoor Plants

From the descriptions of the many different indoor plants already given, it is evident that there are numbers of different aspects of cultivation and environment that have to be considered, if thriving plants are to be enjoyed. The time has now arrived to consider all of them on a practical plane.

Light

The fact is that human beings are able to keep more healthy, or at least they think they can, in less light than plants need. As a result, most places in our homes are not light enough to suit the well-being of many indoor plants. Thus, keeping house plants at their best under such conditions is not an easy task. To start with, it is important to get rid of one assumption that might appear to be logical, but is completely erroneous, and that is that any shortcomings in this respect can be overcome by giving the plants long spells in direct sunshine. With a few exceptions, plants object to being exposed directly to the rays of the sun.

Now those who are dedicated enthusiasts to growing house plants can overcome this difficulty by installing cabinets, racks of shelves, planteriums, all illuminated with fluorescent strip-lighting burning for long hours during the day. Some despise the altering strength of natural light during the day and create a completely independent environment for their house plants in a cellar, where the hours and intensity of light can be rigidly controlled.

Fortunately, the majority of us have house plants in our homes because they are pretty and add considerably to the interior decoration. There are, however, two important things that can be learnt from these house plant enthusiasts and the research work of the plant scientists, that provided them with their expert knowledge. These are, firstly, that the majority of house plants must have good light and secondly, that they appear to be as happy in artificial light as in sunlight. So important is the first point that emphasis is always given to those few plants that will tolerate poor lighting.

There are several things therefore that owners of house plants can do to meet the needs of their plants. The first is to put them always in the lightest place out of the sunshine in the room; secondly, move them as near the window as possible; and thirdly, keep the curtains and blinds fully open as

long as possible during the day. If house plants have to be put into a dark corner, make sure that fluorescent lighting is provided to supplement the natural light. Spotlights have proved very effective for this purpose. It must be remembered that a grouping of house plants in a dark corner of a room has no value as a decorative feature. So light it up.

Warmth

Throughout the book, the necessity of giving plants varying degrees of warmth has been continuously mentioned. Fortunately, in these days of central heating, the heat conditions in many houses is much more suitable for house plants than it was in former days. The big menace is fluctuations of temperature arising from fairly long periods early in the day when rooms are not heated much, then other periods when they might be overheated, followed by a rapid fall in the temperature during the night, perhaps even below freezing point. Such conditions are far more damaging for most plants than their being kept continuously in a steadily cool place. So in order to keep house plants healthy, put them in a position where the temperature is as uniform as possible. Always avoid, for example, standing them on the mantelpiece, where they might be roasted for part of the day, on the shelf over the radiator or, at night, behind the closed curtains on the window-sill, because it is likely to become intensely cold in so restricted an area. Ideally the aim of an indoor gardener is to maintain a continuous day temperature of 60°–70°F (15°–21°C) degrees with a minimum of 45°F (7°C) or a little higher at night. If a plant is caught by the frost, it should be put in a position remote from the fire and sprayed with cold water. It might then return to normal.

Humidity

It is realized by now that a good number of house plants have a preference for high or moderate humidity. This condition is coupled with the temperature and air circulation because in a closed area excessive heat dries the atmosphere to such an extent that it is harmful to many plants. This is therefore another thing to be watched. Control of humidity in a living-room is difficult. If it is overdone, some plants might revel in it, but human beings cannot stand it. Moist air is, however, more important to many house plants than warmth. So, if success is to be attained, it is necessary to provide humidity in the vicinity of the plants themselves. There are two principal ways in which this can be done. The first is to put the plant in its original pot in another rather larger one (which might well have a decorated exterior), and to pack the space on the bottom and sides with moist peat, which is kept continuously moist. (See Figure 6.) The second is to use a pebble tray. This consists of a tray or dish half filled with pebbles on which the

Keeping the air humid
Opposite: Figure 6 (left)
Figure 7 (middle)
Figure 8 (far left)

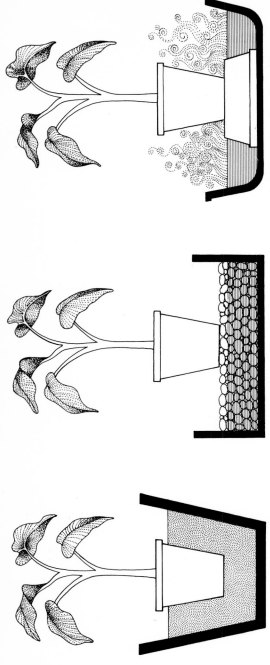

pot is stood. Water is added to nearly cover the stones. This is topped up from time to time to compensate for evaporation loss. (See Figure 7.) Some plants, such as *cyclamen, persicum* and saintpaulia, respond well to a periodic steam bath. This is given by placing an upturned seed pan or block of wood at the bottom of a washing-up bowl and pouring into it boiling water to a level just below the top of the pan or block. The pot is stood on this platform for five minutes and then re-turned to its usual quarters. (See Figure 8.)

Syringing or spraying the foliage, particularly in hot weather, assists in maintaining a high level of humidity.

The Importance of Fresh Air

Fresh air, *without draughts*, is particularly beneficial to house plants. It clears the house of gas and other fumes.

Watering

Like all other plants, indoor plants must have water available at their roots in order to absorb nutriment from the soil and to enable them to manufacture their needs of starch (*Photosynthesis*). The problem that many owners of house plants have to face is when to water. It is very difficult to give a clear solution to this because so much depends on the nature of the plant, the season of year and the environment in which it lives. Plants with fleshy leaves, such as cacti and succulents, do not require as much watering as the plants with thinner leaves, because they are able to retain water within their tissues. On the other hand, plants with proportionately large leaves require more frequent watering, because they have a larger surface from which the plant breathes out water vapour. Again, there are generally two distinct periods in the year of the average plant, the season when it is growing fast and another when it is resting. During the first it needs plenty of watering, and this should normally tail off until the dormant period is reached, when the amount of water given should be quite small. Another important factor is the conditions under which a house plant is living. When the temperature is high and the light is bright, its demand for water is high. A plant kept continuously in a cool place requires much less frequent watering. Also a plant habitually needs more frequent watering if it is in a well-drained pot. If it is in a clay pot, from which the rate of evaporation is higher, it needs more watering than when it is planted in a plastic one. Plants in small pots and those that are becoming pot-bound also need more watering. On the other hand, newly re-potted ones and those in large pots should be treated more cautiously. It is difficult to lay down any hard and fast rules. Generally, however, it is better to under-water *slightly* rather than give excess, to allow the soil, which is darker in colour when it is moist, to dry out to a considerable extent before watering is repeated, and to give plenty of water during the spring and summer, i.e. the growing season, and little during the winter, i.e. the resting period. It is advantageous to use water with the chill off and perhaps, rather more difficult, according to some experts, to give rainwater or softened water, but in most cases it is not harmful to use tapwater.

Each watering must be thorough with a fairly long interval in between; a daily dribble is valueless. Because of the possibility of chilling when the temperature falls at night, house plants should be watered in the morning during the winter. In summer they should not be watered in direct sunshine as any water falling on them is likely to scorch the leaves.

Watering can be done in most cases, either by plunging the pots in water up to half their depths and allowing them to stay there until the soil is fairly moist, but on no account waterlogged. The water is absorbed by capillary action. After this, the pots should be drained and put back in their place. The other alternative is watering from above, in which case it is important to be sure that there is a space of at least one inch between the rim and the level of the soil, and to use a small watering can with a long, narrow spout, that can be inserted between the leaves so that they do not get wetted. It is important to remember, however, that some plants, such as cyclamen and saintpaulia, can be seriously damaged by having their leaves, stalks, and growing centres splashed. These must be watered from below. Unless they are aquatic plants, such as *Cyperus diffusum* or great moisture lovers such as *Helxine soleirolii* (Mind Your Own Business), house plants should never stand permanently in water in a saucer.

Methods such as packing wet peat around pots and standing them in pebble trays, have already been discussed on page 133 under 'Humidity'. These can help where the demand for water is very high, or if watering can only be carried out infrequently, or when the owner is away on holiday, of maintaining an adequate level of moisture. In addition, there are automatic self-watering and wick-watering pots on the market that are useful for emergencies, but none of these devices is a real substitute for personal attention. There are also inexpensive instruments available for indicating when water is necessary, but valuable as they are, their use must be tempered with experience.

Cleaning and Polishing Leaves

Plants grown indoors do not have their leaves washed regularly by the rain like their outdoor counterparts. Since the leaves play such an important role in maintaining health, it is necessary to see that their pores are kept free from dust and smoke grime, and that a film does not form on their surfaces which will reduce the amount of light reaching them. Although perhaps nowadays, with centrally-heated rooms and electric fires, this is not such a major problem, it is still necessary to keep the foliage clean and, of course, it improves the plant's appearance. Both the upper and lower surfaces of the leaves should be sponged with tepid water and if they are very dirty, soapy water can be used, but it must be thoroughly rinsed off afterwards. Plants with finely cut and delicate foliage must be cleansed by thorough spraying. Some people like to give the leaves a good shine, but olive oil, which does achieve this end quite effectively, tends to attract the dust, especially in the pores where it is easily lodged. There is, however, a proprietary aqueous wax emulsion that appears to be quite safe and that gives a shine lasting for months.

Feeding

There are no differences in the nutritional requirements of house plants from those of the multitude that grow in the open. When plants are first purchased they are usually fertilized for some months, but thereafter they benefit from small regular doses of a solution of a proprietary liquid manure (there are several especially blended for house plants), that can be given at the time of watering. Foliage and summer-flowering house plants should be fed during the summer and the winter-flowering ones in the winter. No plants should be fed during their resting time, otherwise they will be undesirably forced.

Re-potting

This is an operation to be postponed as long as possible because most house plants flourish best in what appears to be too small a pot. The day does come, however, when they are pot-bound. This is normally indicated by the slowing up of growth, rapid drying out of the soil and roots growing through the drainage hole. It can be confirmed by knocking out the root ball. If it consists mainly of a matted mass of visible roots and little soil, then the plant needs re-potting.

The pot chosen for this purpose should be the next size larger, perhaps two sizes larger in the case of a vigorous grower. If it is a clay one, a layer of crocks should cover the drain hole. This should be followed by a thin layer of peat, followed by another of potting compost. The plant is then removed from its old pot. The old crocks are taken away from the base of its root ball and a few of the matted outside roots loosened without disturbing the root ball. It is placed on top of the compost in the new pot and the space round it gradually filled, with gentle firming, with slightly moist compost until the level of the base of the stem is reached, which should be about an inch below the rim of the pot. After finally tapping the pot down several times, it is watered, placed in a shady place for a week and sprayed daily. After this, it can be put back in its usual quarters.

A good compost for this purpose is a mixture of two parts commercial potting compost and one part garden peat. In addition, there are nowadays several proprietary soilless composts that are recommended for this purpose.

In the case of very large house plants re-potting is difficult to do with safety. The difficulty can be overcome by *top-dressing*, which consists of removing in the spring the top one to two inches of the soil from the pot, without disturbing the roots, and replacing it with a commercial potting compost with which has been mixed a little commercial base fertilizer.

House Plants during Holidays

House plants, like pets, must be considered at holiday time. Most people do not really want to bother their neighbours at such times. If the plants are thoroughly watered beforehand, they can be left in a cool place quite satisfactorily for the duration of a short holiday. If the holiday is rather more prolonged, the pots can be surrounded with moist peat, or stood on a water-filled pebble tray (see page 133). For such periods automatic watering equipment is useful. If the weather is warm, each plant after watering can be placed, pot first, into a polythene bag of suitable size and the top open edges closed by twisting together and binding them with transparent tape.

Indoor Plants in Trouble

Indoor plants, just as their outdoor counterparts, are likely to be infested with pests and be attacked by disease. The indoor gardener can nevertheless do quite a lot towards com-

Danger signals shown by indoor plants in trouble

Distress signals	Possible causes
Slow growth	In summer, over-watering or under-feeding. In winter, there is nothing wrong if this is the plant's normal resting time. Might need re-potting.
Wilting	Excessive drying. Over-watering or bad drainage. In too sunny or hot a position. Rotting of the root, if soil wet.
Flowers, buds and leaves falling	As buds are mostly formed in good light, turning the pot so that they are twisted away from it, might cause them to fall. All three might fall because of fluctuations in temperature and light intensity, excessive draught, low humidity, gas fumes, soil dryness and over-watering.
Leaves turn yellow and straggly growth	Over-watering or being kept too dark or too warm in winter. Lack of fertility or light in summer. Might need re-potting.
Leaves turn yellow and fall	Over-watering, cold draughts, low humidity, too low a temperature, gas fumes, or attack by red spider mites.
Leaves turn yellow and remain on the plant	Excessive lime in the case of acid soil-loving plants.
Brown tips and spots on foliage	Over-watering, overheating, too near to the fire or a radiator or in the sun—low humidity, draughts, excessive fertilization and scorching by water splashes.
Drooping leaves with wet soil	Rotting of root due to over-watering. Place in a warm place and only water moderately.
Variegated leaves turning green	Lack of light.
Rotting at leaf axils	Due to water remaining at the joint of the leaves and the main stem.

bating the effects of these menaces. If the plants are regularly inspected and the leaves kept clean, any pests can be picked off by hand, when there are only individuals present and before they get a chance to multiply; if any disease is detected in its early stage, timely action can prevent it spreading and becoming serious. Again, if indoor plants are given the environments and conditions that they like, they flourish and are able to meet adversity without difficulty. Unfortunately, even with the very best intentions, it is not always possible to prevent something disastrous happening. For this reason, some of the more common troubles are briefly discussed.

Pests

Aphides (Greenfly). There are few people not familiar with these troublesome insects, which are sap suckers. They cause the leaves and stems to become distorted and cover them with a sticky substance, called honeydew. The odd few can be picked off; if there are more, the plants should be sprayed with malathion or the systemic menazon.

Red Spider Mites. These minute red insects can be detected by the presence of a fine whitish silken web on the undersides of the leaves, where they live. The leaves acquire a metallic, greyish bronze look, become brittle and fall off. Plants kept in a fairly moist atmosphere are not usually attacked. Spray with petroleum white oil emulsion.

White Flies are sap suckers that cause the foliage to become mottled. In the case of serious attacks, the plants should be sprayed with malathion.

Scale Insects. In the presence of these insects, the stems and undersides of the leaves are covered with off-white scales, which are interspersed with areas of mobile orange scales—the young insects. They are best removed with a thin stick, mounted with cotton wool soaked in methylated spirits.

Mealy Bugs, which look like tufts of cotton, feed on the sap, stunting their host's growth and distorting them. They are best treated as described under scale insects.

Diseases

The most common diseases are mildew and rot.

Mildew. The leaves and stems become covered with a white powder and distorted. When mildew is detected, as far as possible the affected parts should be removed. The plant should be sprayed with Karathane. In the event of an attack, a check should be made to see that the plant is being treated in the correct way.

Rot is usually caused by over-watering and water being allowed to remain on leaves, stems and growing centres. Where feasible, the affected parts should be cut off. It can be prevented by not allowing water to remain on the plant. Sometimes a damaged plant can be resuscitated by keeping it fairly warm and only watering it very moderately.

Creating one's own Indoor Plants

It is usually only the most enthusiastic growers who want to raise their own indoor plants. Others like occasionally to propagate a few as a matter of interest. A few house plants become so unruly and ill-shaped after a few years that it is better to replace them periodically, and then, of course, it is more economic to raise their replacements. When contemplating doing this, however, it is important to remember that with plants that have originated in humid, warm semitropical and tropical areas, it is not always possible for many householders without a heated greenhouse to create the conditions necessary for success. On a limited scale, it is possible to root some cuttings and germinate some seeds by covering the compost in which they are planted with a polythene bag, supported on four stakes, inserted in the soil in their pots and tied just below the rims with string, so that they are in a sealed atmosphere. If the compost has been well watered and the hooded container placed in a warm place, the conditions of a heated, humid greenhouse would be reproduced.

Gardeners will be familiar with the more common methods of propagation because indoor plants are multiplied in exactly the same way as those that grow in the open. Anybody who wishes to have more detailed information is recommended to consult gardening books that include propagation.

Raising from Seed. The raising of plants from seeds is normally a simple and easy method of propagation, which most people have tried at some time or another. It is dealt with below, when the more novel subject of raising certain indoor plants from fruit stones and pips is discussed.

Layering. This is particularly easy and is a satisfactory way of propagating some indoor plants, particularly *Chlorophytum*, *Ficus pumila, F. radicans, Gynura sarmentosa* and *Saxifraga sarmentosa*, which send out runners like strawberries, with tufts of leaves growing at their tips. If a slanting incision is made in the stem in the vicinity of this growth, the leaves removed and the growing point pegged down securely in potting compost in another pot, roots will usually form within about five weeks, when the plantlet can be cut off from the parent.

Air layering. This very useful process is discussed in detail on page 50.

Division. Most gardeners are familiar with the method of propagating by division, which is usually applied in the spring to indoor plants in exactly the same way as it is to those growing in the open. It is a particularly valuable method for multiplying *Acorus gramineus, Aspidistra lurida* and *Spathiphyllum wallisii*.

Cuttings. Just as with outdoor plants, there are three types of cuttings that are usually used for propagating indoor plants, viz. stem, heel and leaf. They are all planted as deeply as possible in a rooting medium, such as a commercial potting compost or a soil-less compost. It is important to plant deeply so that the cutting is well firmed in, in order that there is no movement detrimental to the growing of roots. Although it is not essential if the growing qualities of the soil and the conditions are suitable for the plant, the lower ends of the cuttings can be moistened and dipped into a proprietary hormone rooting compound, which facilitates the formation of roots.

Stem Cuttings are taken by cutting a shoot just below a leaf joint, that is, about six inches from its tip, with a sharp knife or razor blade. All the buds and leaves are removed from the lower half and the cutting planted to this depth. The ivies, *Rhoicissus rhomboidea, Cissus antarctica* and some philodendrons are good subjects for this type of propagation. In fact, cuttings of tradescantia, busy lizzie, coleus and ivies will easily form roots if merely stood in a bottle of water.

Heel Cuttings are usually taken from wooded plants. A shoot is torn off the older stem leaving a heel of bark. It is reduced to about six inches in length and all the buds and leaves removed from its lower half, to which depth it should be planted.

Leaf Cuttings. An adult leaf is cut off its point of origin, preferably in the summer or growing season, using a razor blade or sharp knife. The stalk is then inserted as deeply as possible in a rooting medium. Saintpaulias and begonias respond well to this treatment.

Raising Novelties for Indoor Decorations

All of us remember the enormous pleasure we had when, as children, we planted a peach stone against a sunny, warm wall and had the thrill of seeing it develop into a tiny shrub laden with leaves, and how, in later years, we enjoyed its beautiful pink blossoms and, ultimately its luscious fruits. Such happiness does not die easily in one's heart and many

... of us still derive much satisfaction from planting unusual seeds and seeing them mature. The pleasure is so great, that often our enthusiasm inspires our children to follow the same exciting course and to raise some exotic plant, which is unusual and beautiful, and, in doing so, explore the intricacies of Nature's ways of reproducing her kind.

It is remarkable how easily so many of the fruit pips and stones discarded from our meal tables can be persuaded to root themselves and become most attractive house plants. A few of these are discussed in the ensuing paragraphs.

Indoor Plants from Fruit Pips

The more common of the citrus fruits—oranges, lemons, tangerines and grapefruit—will take root and produce the most attractive small trees, if their pips are planted. When selecting the seeds for this purpose, a lookout should be kept for the really plump ones. They can usually be collected at any time of the year. Any of them should be washed thoroughly. It is also an advantage to soften them by a soaking in cold water for a full day. They should then be planted, three to a pot, half an inch to an inch deep, according to their size, in a damp commercial potting compost. Next, it is necessary to cover the potted seeds, either with a polythene bag, as discussed above, or with a large glass jam jar, or the seeds may be planted in one of those more recently introduced propagating pots with a well-fitting transparent, plastic hood.

The pots are then kept in a warm, dark place until the pips germinate. They are then put in a light place and shortly afterwards the transparent covering is removed. When a pair of leaves have appeared, each tiny plant is transplanted into its own six-inch pot in a commercial potting compost. If they are kept in a light position with reasonable warmth, they will develop into attractive little trees with very decorative glossy, dark-green foliage.

Indoor Plants from Fruit Stones

The stones of apricots, avocado pears, dates, lychees, and peaches can be made to produce very charming indoor plants, but they are harder to persuade to root than the pips of citrus fruits. Generally, the initial procedure for raising plants from these seeds is the same as described for the pips. It is as well, however, to plant a few spare date stones because several of them might be infertile. One also has to be patient and keep them in a dark place for a much longer time before they germinate. Two months will pass before there are any signs of date stones germinating, while it might be as long as four months with avocado pears. Allow a few weeks to pass after germination; then the seedlings should be re-potted into three-inch pots, using a commercial potting compost as the growing medium.

Kept warm and well-watered, all these small plants grow up into attractive little trees. It should, however, be appreciated that in its habitat, the avocado pear grows to a height of sixty feet. Thus, despite its beauty, it can eventually become far too tall to be accommodated in a normal house.

Pineapple

A particularly novel plant to grow from scrap is a pineapple. With its silvery, long-toothed, curving foliage, it makes a very beautiful house plant, and at no cost. What is more, if grown in a warm room, it will often fruit two years after planting. The fleshy top with a rosette of healthy leaves is cleanly cut off during the spring when it is being prepared for the table. The lower leaves are removed to uncover about one inch of the bare stump. After it has dried out for a few days, it should be planted in moist sand, tying it to a stake to support it.

It should be placed in a warm, light place and the sand watered when it dries out. The sand should be gently probed about once a fortnight, and as soon as roots appear, the pineapple should be transferred to a small pot in a commercial potting compost. During the summer it should be watered quite abundantly, and transplanted if it becomes rootbound. During the winter, it should still be kept in a warm place, but watering should be much reduced. When spring comes, it should be re-potted and the rate of watering steadily increased. After this the pineapple, which will soon begin to grow a fruit stem, should receive a steady liquid feed.

Bush Plants

Foliage house plants

	Easy to grow	For average rooms in which the lighting is reasonable and which are maintained heated for some hours daily during the winter	Unheated areas (halls, landings and staircases)	Especially suitable for centrally-heated rooms and other continuously warm rooms. (Care must be taken to see that the air surrounding the plants is humid.	Rooms without sun
Acorus gramineus 'Variegatus' (Grass)		●			
Aglaonemas				●	
Aralia (see *Dizygotheca*)					
Araucaria excelsa			●	●	
Aspidistra lurida		●	●	●	●
Aucuba japonica 'Variegata'		●	●	●	
Begonia maculata				●	
B. masoniana				●	
B. rex				●	●
Bromeliads (*Cryptanthus* and *Nidulariums*)	●			●	
Calathea mackoyana				●	
Cordyline (or *Dracaena terminalis*)		●	●	●	
Cyperus diffusus (Grass)	●	●	●	●	
Dieffenbachias				●	
Dizygotheca (*Aralia*) *elegantissima*				●	
Dracaenas				●	
D. sanderi				●	
D. deremensis 'Bausei'				●	
D. fragrans				●	
Fatshedera lizei	●	●	●	●	
Fatsia japonica	●	●	●	●	
Ficus	●	●		●	
Fittonias				●	
Grevillea robusta	●	●	●	●	
Helxine soleirolii	●	●		●	●
Marantas		●		●	
Monstera deliciosa 'Borsigiana'	●	●		●	
Pandanus veitchii				●	
Peperomias		●		●	
Philodendrons		●		●	
Pileas		●		●	
Sansevieria trifasciata 'Laurentii'	●	●		●	
Saxifraga sarmentosa (*stolonifera*)	●	●	●	●	
Schefflera actinophylla	●	●	●	●	
Setcreasea purpurea	●	●			●
Tolmiea menziesii	●	●	●	●	●

* This is best done by placing them on wet pebble trays or packing them in wet peat.

Plants that withstand fumes, e.g. gas, cooking, tobacco, etc.

Plants for flower arrangers

Large plants suitable for offices and large spaces

(Some)

(F. elastica 'Decora')
(F. lyrata)

(P. bipinnatifidum)
(P. erubescens)

Small plants suitable for limited areas

(Cryptantus)

Suitable for dark rooms and full shade

(F. elastica 'Decora')

Plants that flourish in full sun

Climbers and Trailers

Foliage Plants	Easy to grow	For average rooms in which the light is reasonable, and there is some sunshine, and which are maintained heated for some hours daily.	Unheated areas (halls, landings and staircases)	Especially suitable for centrally-heated rooms and other continuously warm rooms. (Care must be taken to see that the air surrounding the plants is humid.)	Rooms without sun
Chlorophytum capense 'Variegatum'	●	●		●	
Cissus antarctica	●	●			
C. discolor	●	●	●	●	
Ficus pumila	●	●	●	●	
Hederas	●	●		●	
Philodendron melanochryson (andreanum)		●		●	
P. scandens	●	●	●	●	
Rhoicissus rhomboidea	●	●		●	
Scindapsus aureus	●	●	●	●	
Syngonium podophyllum (nephthytis)		●		●	
Tetrastigma voinerianum					
Tradescantias	●	●		●	
Zebrina pendula	●	●		●	

Flowering Plants	Easy to grow	For average rooms in which the light is reasonable, and there is some sunshine, and which are maintained heated for some hours daily.	Unheated areas (halls, landings and staircases)	Especially suitable for centrally-heated rooms and other continuously warm rooms. (Care must be taken to see that the air surrounding the plants is humid.)	Rooms without sun
Campanula isophylla			●	●	
Cobaea scandens				●	
Columnea banksii				●	●
Hoya bella			●	●	
Jasminum polyanthum			●		●
Aechmeas		●		●	
Anthurium scherzerianum				●	
Aphelandras				●	
Beloperone guttata	●		●	●	●
Bilbergia nutans	●		●	●	
Callistemon citrinus			●	●	
Clivia miniata	●		●	●	●
Guzmanias				●	
Hoya carnosa			●	●	●
Impatiens petersiana	●		●	●	●
Saintpaulia ionantha			●	●	●
Spathiphyllum wallisii					●
Vriesia splendens			●	●	

Plants that withstand fumes, e.g. gas, cooking, tobacco, etc.

Plants for flower arrangers

Large plants suitable for offices and large spaces

Small plants suitable for limited areas

Suitable for dark rooms and full shade

Plants that flourish in full sun

Index

Acknowledgements

The following colour transparencies by courtesy of:

Bernard Alfieri Natural History Photographic Agency: 52; 64 right; 81 left; 81 bottom left & right; 84–85; 92 right; 92 bottom right; 124 above

A–Z Botanical Collection: 57; 64 bottom left

Camera Press London: 15; 18–19; 22–23; 88

W. F. Davidson: 49; 81 below left

Dobies of Chester: 96 below left; 96 bottom right

J. E. Downward: 89; 93; 96 bottom left

Peter Hunt: 11; 30; 31; 81 bottom right

Jackson & Perkins: 6–7; 14; 26; 53; 116–117; 121; 125; 128

E. A. Over: 113 below left; below right; bottom left; bottom right

Harry Smith: 27; 56; 60; 61; 64 below right; 64 bottom right; 92 below left; 92 below right; 92 bottom left; 120

Spectrum: 10

Syndication International: 124 below

The following black and white photographs by courtesy of:

Bernard Alfieri (NHPA): 32 below right; 34; 35 left; 37; 39 below; 40; 42 right; 42 below left; 44 below right; 47; 48 bottom right; 50 below; 54–55; 58 top left; 58 top right; 58 middle right; 58 bottom left; 59 below left; 63; 68 below; 69 below; 71; 78 below left;

80 left; 97; 102; 104; 105; 106 below; 108 below; 109; 110 above; 110 below; 111 above; 112 below; 112 right; 114 above; 115 left; 115 bottom right; 123 below left; 134; 137

Conway: 16; 20; 28

Dalton: 8; 12; 50 right; 50 bottom right; 62 right; 69 bottom left; 72 below left; 74 below; 103; 115 bottom left

J. E. Downward: 21; 24; 32 right; 32 below left; 35 below; 36 below left; right; 38 below left & right; 39 left; 39 bottom left; 41 below left; right; 41 bottom left; 42 below left & right; 42 below right; 46 bottom right; 48 below left; 48 below right; 51 below left; 51 below right; 58 middle left; 59 below right; 62 below left; 62 bottom right; 66 below; right; 67; 69 left; 69 bottom right; 70 right; 70 below; 72 below right; 73 left; 74 below right; 76; 77; 78 left; 79 left & right; 80 below left & right; 82 below; 82 bottom; 83; 86; 90 below; 90 right; 91; 94; 106 right; 106 bottom left & right; 108 right; 112 bottom left & right; 114 below; 118; 122; 123 below right; 123 bottom; 126; 129 left;

Peter Hunt: 13; 46 below right; 62 below; 99; 100; 130; 131

George Hyde: 101

Lavinia Press: 4

Harry Smith: 42 bottom left; 46 below left; 51 left; 58 bottom left; 66 below left; 73 right; 111 below; 115 right; 129 right

Syndication International: 1